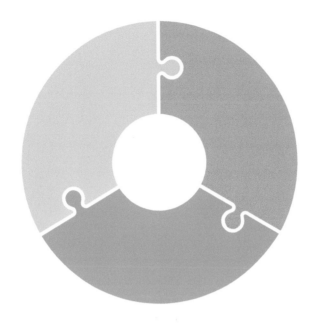

SOCIAL-EMOTIONAL LEADERSHIP

A Guide for Youth Development

• • •

Micela Leis
Susan Reinecke

978-1-60491-975-2 – Print

978-1-60491-976-9 – Ebook

CCL No. 001008

Published by the Center for Creative Leadership
CCL Press

Authors: Micela Leis, Susan Reinecke

Editor: Shaun Martin

Rights and Permissions: Kelly Lombardino

https://www.ccl.org/permission-republish-request/

Design and Layout: Carly Bell, Ed Morgan

CONTENTS

Introduction · 6

Part 1: Leading Self · 15

  1. Self-Aware · 17
  2. Accountable · 31
  3. Resilient · 41
  4. Integrity · 53

Part 2: Leading with Others · 65

  5. Collaborative · 67
  6. Communicative · 81
  7. Active Listener · 91
  8. Considerate · 103
  9. Respectful · 113
  10. Accepting · 123

Part 3: Changing Your World · 133

  11. Visionary · 135
  12. Motivating · 145
  13. Encouraging · 157
  14. Confident · 167

Conclusion · 178

About the Authors · 179

Acknowledgments · 180

About the Center for Creative Leadership · 181

INTRODUCTION

Imagine walking into a classroom where students are deeply engaged in learning. There is an atmosphere of respect, trust, and collaboration. Whether individually or in groups, students actively challenge themselves and support each other. In this imagined classroom, the teacher provides individual attention to a student or to a small group of students, while remaining confident that the rest of the class will stay on task. Now step back for a moment. What you are observing is a classroom where students are consistently displaying social-emotional leadership: They are in charge of themselves and their own actions (Leading Self), and they are working well with their classmates (Leading with Others) on important projects for their learning and growth (Changing Your World).

By focusing on developing a student's social-emotional leadership, you can start to create classrooms like the one we've described. [For consistency, we use the term students throughout this book to refer to youth under the age of 18. Likewise, we use the term educators to refer to any adults who work with youth. This does not mean that this book is meant specifically for school settings.] Youth need to be competent in leadership attributes such as resilience, communication, and collaboration, and they need to have the ability to engage and motivate others in order to face the complex challenges of the 21st century (Ananiadou, 2009; Geisinger, 2016). Research conducted by the Center for Creative Leadership (CCL) finds that student leadership is related to engagement with school and with more positive academic and social-emotional outcomes (DePass, Ehrlich, & Leis, 2019).

The Student Leadership Framework

In order to develop student leadership, it is necessary to understand what student leadership is and what it looks like. We define it this way: *Student leadership is about building the capacity of all young people to have a greater impact on themselves, their peers, and their world.* Based on multi-year, mixed-methods research with teachers, parents, administrators, and over 10,000 students in grades 3–12 in public and private schools in multiple states, CCL has developed a framework for defining student leadership (Leis, Leisman, Ehrlich, & Kosovich, 2018) and a scale for measuring it (Leis, Leisman, Kosovich, & Ehrlich, 2018).

This Student Leadership Framework describes the 14 leadership attributes (*see Table 1*) that are central to student leadership. These are organized into the following three distinct dimensions:[1]

- **Leading Self** – deep understanding of yourself and your own behavior
- **Leading with Others** – working effectively with others
- **Changing Your World** – working to make a positive impact in the world

Each dimension is comprised of three to six attributes (described in Table 1).

Table 1: Student Leadership Framework Attributes and Definitions

DIMENSIONS	ATTRIBUTES	DEFINITIONS
Leading Self	Self-Aware	can describe what makes them who they are
	Accountable	takes responsibility for their actions
	Resilient	keeps trying if they fail at an important goal
	Integrity	stands up for what they believe in
Leading with Others	Collaborative	cooperates with others effectively
	Communicative	expresses ideas clearly and effectively
	Active Listener	listens carefully to what others have to say
	Considerate	thinks about how their actions make other people feel
	Respectful	treats other people the way they want to be treated
	Accepting	appreciates the views of others, even if they are different from their own
Changing Your World	Visionary	creates a compelling vision and inspires others to follow it
	Motivating	unites a group of people to work together toward a common goal
	Encouraging	encourages others to take on leadership roles
	Confident	steps up and takes charge when it is needed

This book describes each of these attributes in detail and also provides discussion questions, journal prompts, and sample activities that can be adapted for different ages and contexts to spur student leadership development in your school or youth organization—at your pace and according to your priorities.

Who This Book Is For, What's in This Book, and Why It's Important

This book is for teachers, principals, guidance counselors, parents, and others looking to develop student leadership. Student leadership requires students to understand themselves and work with others to accomplish their goals and change the world around them. The information and ideas in this book helps educators understand and explain the 14 attributes described in the Student Leadership Framework to the students with whom they work. This book also includes discussion questions, sample activities, and journal prompts to help educators build student capacity in these attributes. The attributes themselves are a distillation of the characteristics, actions, and perspectives that are at the heart of student leadership.

How This Book Is Organized

Each chapter in this book discusses one of the 14 important leadership attributes described in the Student Leadership Framework. Each of the book's chapters includes the following sections:

- **Introduction.** This section includes a simple description of the attribute, what mastery of the attribute looks like, and common obstacles to development.

- **Suggestions for Improvement.** This section provides suggestions for building competency in the specific attribute.

- **Activity Center.** This section provides suggestions of different activities that can be used in group settings to help students develop skills in this attribute. These activities may be modified for the students with whom you work.

- **Journal Prompts.** This section provides journal prompts that can be given to students to stimulate reflection on the attribute. Choose or modify journal prompts to make them developmentally appropriate.

- **Integrating the Attribute into Your Curriculum.** This section provides questions that can be used to facilitate conversation about the attribute with students.

- **Questions to Assess Understanding.** This section provides questions that can be given to students to assess their understanding of the attribute. We recommend that these questions be used developmentally, rather than in an evaluative manner. That is, they should be used as a tool to check in on a student's understanding of the attribute, rather than as a graded assessment of their comprehension.

- **Suggested Books to Introduce the Attribute.** This section provides titles of picture books that may be used to deepen younger students' understanding of the attributes.

- **Additional Resources.** This section provides additional places to look for help and advice to develop your personal knowledge, as an adult, about this attribute.

How to Use This Book

Use this book as a guide for improving and developing student leadership skills. Each chapter focuses on a unique attribute, allowing you to organize your student leadership development efforts. This book also makes an excellent companion to the *Leadership Indicator for Students* (LIS). For more information on the LIS see page 12.

Use the resources in each chapter to create a lesson to use with your students. Though there is no right way to craft a lesson, we suggest the following: Use the information in the chapter's introductory text to familiarize students with the topic. You might use the question stem "How does this attribute make you a better leader?" to start a discussion with your students and to check for comprehension (see Additional Resources for more information to further your personal understanding). Work with students to discuss and establish some ways that people can become skilled in the attribute (see Suggestions for Improvement for sample strategies).

Have students participate in an activity (see *Activity Center* for suggestions) or ask them to write about the attribute (see *Journal Prompts*). Incorporate the attribute into your own curriculum through debriefing conversations (see *Integrating the Attribute into Your Curriculum*). Additional ways to integrate the attributes into day-to-day classroom work may include:

- Create an "Improving Leadership" contract with students and have everyone sign it. Display this contract in the classroom and refer students' attention to it to reinforce working on the leadership behavior.

- Conduct daily or weekly check-ins where students can share how they have been working on developing this attribute.

- Assign accountability partners for each student to monitor and give feedback on each other's progress. (An accountability partner is someone students can trust to offer honest feedback and support and keep them on track to meet their goals.)

- Create a praise box. Students write down when they see another student working to become more skilled in this attribute and put it in the praise box. Decide how to share the praise in a way that works best for you and your students.

Consider using the written Questions to Assess Understanding as formative student assessment to determine if you need to spend more time explaining this attribute. Other ways to incorporate social-emotional leadership concepts in your day-to-day work may include:

- add comprehension questions about the attribute to a project rubric

- have students keep an observational journal in which they write about how others display the attributes

- have the students create online portfolios in which they reflect on how they are developing their social-emotional leadership

- noting student development in the attributes and sharing this information with parents and guardians

Norms for Discussions and Activities

Developing personal leadership attributes can be challenging, as students are asked to be deeply reflective, vulnerable, and transparent. In order to facilitate this process, it may be helpful to share the following norms:

- assume positive intent

- respect each other

- listen for understanding

- speak for yourself, not others

- speak about yourself, not others

- know when to step up and when to step back

- stay open to others' opinions

- meet people where they are

- allow and support all voices to be heard

Notes

[1] The original Student Leadership Framework contains a fourth dimension: **Leading Academically**, which is defined as the belief that learning is important and valuable. Three attributes comprise this dimension: 1) **Values school** (*believes school is important for future outcomes*), 2) **Participative** (*participates in class/group discussions*), and 3) **Attentive** (*pays attention when the teacher is speaking*). While CCL's research identifies this dimension as an important aspect of student leadership, we do not focus on it in this book for two reasons: 1) development of the other leadership attributes described in the framework contribute to strengthening this dimension, and 2) educators already constantly and consistently focus their efforts in this area.

References

Ananiadou, K. & Claro, M. (2009). 21st century skills and competences for new millennium learners in OECD countries. *OECD Education Working Papers, 41.* http://dx.doi.org/10.1787/218525261154

DePass, M., Ehrlich, V., & Leis, M. (2019). Accelerating school success: Transforming K–12 schools by investing in leadership development. White paper. Greensboro, NC: Center for Creative Leadership.

Geisinger, K. F. (2016). 21st century skills: What are they and how do we assess them? *Applied Measurement in Education, 29*(4), 245–249.

Leis., M., Leisman, T., Ehrlich, V., & Kosovich, J. J. (2018). *Understanding and measuring leadership from a student perspective: Creation and validation of the student leadership scale (SLS).* Poster presented at the meeting of the Society for Research on Educational Effectiveness, Washington, DC.

Leis, M., Leisman, T., Kosovich, J., & Ehrlich, V. (2018). *Leadership indicator for students* (LIS) technical manual. Greensboro, NC: Center for Creative Leadership.

The Leadership Indicator for Students (LIS)

The LIS, developed in conjunction with CCL's evidence-based Student Leadership Framework, is a tool for assessing student leadership development needs within a school or youth organization. The LIS comprehensively examines student leadership through three different perspectives:

- students' perception of **themselves**

- students' perceptions of their **peers**

- teachers' perceptions of their **students**

This assessment highlights the gaps between the leadership attributes that the school or youth organization identifies as most important and students' strengths in those attributes. The LIS reveals the top five attributes on which to focus student leadership development efforts for your specific school or organization. These attributes are aligned with the attributes described in this book.

LEADING SELF

In order to lead with others, you must first understand how to lead yourself. This includes being aware of your strengths and challenges and being committed to self-improvement. This section includes information about the following leadership attributes:

ATTRIBUTES	DEFINITIONS
Self-Aware	can describe what makes them who they are
Accountable	takes responsibility for their actions
Resilient	keeps trying if they fail at an important goal
Integrity	stands up for what they believe in

"Leading Self means that I am self-aware of what is happening and how I feel. It means that I am growth-minded and open to new ideas. It means that I am motivated in what I do. It means that I am resilient. It means that I am accountable."

– Middle School Student

Chapter 1
SELF-AWARE

• • •

"Being self-aware is being able to control what you say and who you say it to."
– Eighth Grade Student

"I am aware of both my negative and positive qualities and the areas where I am capable and the areas where I need help."
– 12th Grade Student

Introduction

Explaining "Self-Aware" to Students

We all have a mental picture of ourselves—what we believe, how we treat others, what we are good at, and what we may not be so good at. But do you see yourself as others see you? If you asked someone else to describe you, could you accurately predict what that person would say? **To be self-aware means understanding who you are, your strengths, and areas in which you can improve.** It's important to understand not only how we see ourselves but also how others see us. Why do you think that is? One reason is that if you understand the areas in which you need to improve, you can ask for help in these areas from other people. Asking for help will allow you to build relationships and work well with others, which is very important for leadership.

What "Self-Aware" Looks Like

Self-aware leaders:

- have an accurate picture of their strengths and weaknesses

- are aware of their feelings

- reflect on and learn from experience

- seek feedback to improve

- are open to criticism and can hear feedback without getting defensive

- work on what they need to learn

- respond well to new situations that require them to stretch and grow

- know what their values are and why they are important to them

- are seen as authentic, attentive, thoughtful, responsive, reflective, and observant

- know how their actions affect others

- adjust their behavior to suit circumstances

What Gets in the Way?

When you are not self-aware, you might see yourself differently than others see you. This may lead to your misreading different situations and not acting appropriately. Your actions can contribute to confusion, frustration, and feelings of being misunderstood. Review the following list and note the items that might give you trouble developing self-awareness.

- You don't take time to think about how your actions may affect others.

  » (Examples: gossiping, bullying, not sharing, taking someone else's things, etc.)

- You don't want others to give you feedback.

- You don't believe you have any room for improvement.

- You think your needs are more important than anyone else's.

- You respond defensively to feedback.

- People are afraid to tell you things because they don't want to hurt or offend you.

- You act as if you are someone you are not.

- You have a hard time accepting compliments or positive feedback.

Being able to recognize the positive and negative impact that your words and actions have on others will make you a better social-emotional leader.

Suggestions for Improving "Self-Aware" ——————

Work with your students to discuss and establish some ways to build competency in this attribute. Below is a list to help support this exercise. We encourage you to develop your own strategies or modify these suggestions.

You might also consider doing an activity with your students (see this chapter's Activity Center for suggestions) or asking them to write about the attribute (see Journal Prompts for suggestions) to help build their understanding. Support is an important part of development, so discuss with your students how you can support each other, as a group or class, to build skill in this leadership attribute.

- **Check your awareness.** List the characteristics or descriptions of how you hope others see you. For example: kind, considerate, respectful, fun to be around, optimistic, hard-worker, stands up for what you believe in, dependable. Then, ask your accountability partner to write out a list of how they see you. Compare the lists. If your lists do not match, think about ways that you can act that show how you want others to see you.

- **Reflect on your personal values.** What do you value the most? Where are you willing to compromise? Some of your values are more important to you than others. Think about how your values compare to the values of your family, friends, school, and community.

- **Notice how others respond to your actions.** If other people respond to your actions in unexpected ways, use that information to think about where your self-awareness may be lacking. Journal about what you might be doing or not doing that might lead to these unexpected responses. Ask a trusted friend or family member for feedback.

- **Ask for feedback, and think of it as a gift.** What other people tell you about how they see you will help you be more self-aware. Ask others for feedback, listen without being defensive, thank the people who give you feedback, and think of how you can use the feedback to change your actions.

- **See change as an opportunity.** You can change the beliefs others hold about you and the expectations that they have for your behavior. To make these changes, work on your actions, your approach to different situations, and your understanding about what others need.

- **Note how you respond in times of stress.** How do you act when you are feeling a lot of pressure or when you are in stressful situations? Every difficult situation or challenge is an opportunity for you to reflect on your experience and grow from it. Take time to think back on the activities of your day, the actions you took, and the choices you made. Decide what changes you can make to react differently in the future.

———— Activity Center ————

Here are some suggested activities you can modify to fit your context and the students with whom you work.

- **Book introduction.** Find a book to read with students that has a character who either demonstrates the "self-aware" attribute or who would have benefitted from being more self-aware, and have students discuss or journal about the character's behavior (see the Suggested Books section of this chapter for some books that fit this activity).

- **Verbal self-portrait.** Ask students work with a partner to use words to create a portrait of how they see themselves in terms of their values or actions and how they see their partner (for example: *kind, considerate, helps others when they are sad*). After they've shared their portraits with each other, ask students to divide a piece of paper in half by drawing a line and to create two more self-portraits with words. One of these self-portraits should reflect the title, "This is who I am," and the other, "This is who I want to be." Ask students to think about whether they were surprised about anything their partner wrote about them.

- **Monologue or poem.** Ask students to write a poem or a monologue titled either "This is Who I Am" or "This is Where I Come From" to share with the class. For an example, see George Ella Lyon's poem "Where I'm From," which you can access at: http://www.georgeellalyon.com/where.html.

- **Johari window.** Give students (recommended for students age 16 and older) the Johari Window activity (p. 23). Have them complete their Johari Window with help from a peer or mentor (Luft & Ingham, 1955)

- **Social identity.** Give students the Social Identity prompt (p. 24) to write about and then discuss as a class. You can also structure this activity as a class discussion, working through each question as a group (Hannum, 2007).

- **Values Explorer.** Give students the opportunity to identify and rank their values and create a leader philosophy. You can access a free online version, the CCL ValueAble Leader Tool at https://www.valueableleaderproject.com/.

Johari Window

The Johari Window is a tool to organize your self-awareness. It is a two-by-two grid, with the four parts representing what is known and unknown about you to other people and what is known and unknown about you to yourself. As the figure below shows, what is known about you to others is public, while what is known to you but unknown to others is private. What is not known to you and others is unknowable and therefore not relevant. Most interesting is the quadrant representing what is known by others but not by you. When such information is revealed, when we get blindsided by how others really see us, it has the potential to create dramatic change. We discover a truth about ourselves.

These blindside moments are rare and precious gifts. They hurt—the truth often does—but they also instruct. A good mentor can help you identify these "truths." Ask a peer, parent, or mentor for input for your Johari Window, especially in filling in the top-left quadrant that identifies your blind spots—what you are unaware of but that others know may prevent you from accurately assessing your own behavior and performance.

	Known to Self	Unknown to Self
Known to Others	Examples: • Friendly • Helpful • Curious What you and others know about you	Examples: • Patient • Accepting • Curious What others know about you but you are not aware of
Unknown to Others	Examples: • Lacks confidence • Creative • Religious What you don't let others see	Examples: • Assertive • Visionary • Resilient What you and others don't know about you (Hidden Potential)

Source: Luft, J., & Ingham, H. (1955). The Johari Window, a graphic model of interpersonal awareness. *Proceedings of the Western Training Laboratory in Group Development*. Los Angeles, CA: UCLA.

Social Identity

Directions: Read the following questions and write your answers on a separate sheet of paper.

We all make assumptions about our own identity and that of others. Unfortunately, when we work together, assumptions are often treated as reality. These assumptions influence our beliefs about how others think and the motives for their actions.

Social identity comprises the parts of your identity that come from belonging to particular groups. We use social identity to categorize people into groups, identify with certain groups ourselves, and compare various groups—typically thinking more highly of our own. Use the following questions to work through some of your assumptions. You may wish to keep a particular person in mind (someone you've just met or someone you have problems with) when answering.

- When you are building a relationship with a new friend, what do you want to know about the other person? What do you notice first? Are you attracted to certain characteristics?

- What assumptions do you make about other people based on their social identity? (For example, their religion, the clothes they wear, the sports teams they support, etc.)

- If someone else were describing your identity, what do you think they would notice first? What would be most relevant to them? Why?

- What assumptions do you think other people make about you based on your social identity?

- How much do you think you have in common with other students in your school?

- What do you think makes you different compared to other students in your school?

- What insights occurred as you responded to these questions?

Your awareness of social identity—both yours and that of others—can help you see that people are different from one another, but each person can maintain their group identity while also valuing the contributions of others from different groups. What do you think you need to do next?

Journal Prompts

Choose one or more of the following journal prompts appropriate for the age level you work with. Feel free to modify or extend the prompt. Give students time to reflect on the questions in a personal journal. To extend the exercise, ask students to share their reflections with a peer or small group.

- Think about a time when somebody responded in an unexpected way to something you did. Describe the situation. Why was the response unexpected? Where do you think your self-awareness might have been lacking in this situation? Reflect on what you were doing, or not doing, that might have led to that unexpected response.

- What are your personal values? What are you willing to do to reach your goals? Where are you willing to compromise? Which values are more important to you than others? How do your values compare to the values supported by your school, or the values held by your classmates?

- How does it make you feel to get feedback? How do you react? How do you think you should react? What are some strategies that you could use to be more receptive to feedback?

- How do you think other people see you? How do you want to be seen by others? How can you change your actions and your approach to different situations to allow others to see you the way you wish to be seen?

- Think about the values shown by the actions of one of your good friends or family members. Describe similar values that you have that you might show in different ways. (For example, students who value family may work long hours after school to provide what their family needs, while other students may not work so they have more time to spend with their family.)

- How do you respond in stressful situations? How do you react when you are under pressure? Every challenge is an opportunity when you reflect on your experience and grow from it. Take the time to think back on the activities of your day, the actions you took, and the choices you made; then, decide what changes you could make in the future that could improve the outcome.

- Is there anything about yourself that you are unwilling to admit to others? How might you come to terms with that characteristic so you can acknowledge it but not dwell on it? How might things be different for you if you could acknowledge that characteristic?

Integrating the Attribute into Your Curriculum

Choose an activity from your planning guide or syllabus. After your students complete the activity, relate the activity back to the "self-aware" attribute with a debriefing conversation. Below are suggested questions. Choose or modify questions based on your students' developmental level, your activity, and your context.

This debrief can take the form of a full-group discussion. Consider giving students time to reflect on their answers with partners or in small groups before asking them to share responses with the larger group. Alternatively, ask students to work in small groups to record their responses on flip charts, and then create a gallery walk in which students walk around the room and read what other students have written. If you use a gallery walk, consider asking students to add their own thoughts to the charted responses.

- How did the activity help you understand the attribute "self-aware"?

- How did you work on being self-aware during this activity?

- How did other students demonstrate being self-aware during the activity?

- What does it mean to be self-aware?

- Why is it important to be self-aware?

- How can being self-aware make you a better social-emotional leader?

- How can lack of self-awareness affect leadership?

- How can self-awareness be developed?

- What are some ways you could practice self-awareness moving forward?

- How will you demonstrate self-awareness in your interactions with others?

- What effect can increasing your self-awareness have on you?

- Identify a person, past or present, who demonstrates self-awareness. What specific actions demonstrate that person's self-awareness?

- Identify a book or movie character who demonstrates self-awareness. What specific actions does this character take that demonstrate being self-aware?

Questions to Assess Understanding

Consider giving the following questions to students to determine if you need to spend more time explaining this attribute.

- What does it mean to be self-aware? Give an example of someone you know who shows self-awareness. How does this person demonstrate being self-aware?

- What are three things you are going to work on in order to become more self-aware?

Suggested Books to Introduce "Self-Aware"

The books listed below can be used to deepen younger students' understanding of the "self-aware" attribute.

- *I Like Me!* by N. Carlson

- *The Color Monster* by A. Llenas

- *The Dot* by P. Reynolds

- *It's Okay to Be Different* by T. Parr

- *The Magnificent Me* by D. Haseltine

- *Mommy Doesn't Know My Name* by S. Williams & A. Shachat

- *Red: A Crayon's Story* by M. Hall

- *Sometimes I Feel Like a Mouse* by J. Modesitt

- *Talking Treasure: Stories to Help Build Emotional Intelligence and Resilience in Young Children* by V. Hankin & N. Yuval

- *Today I Feel Silly* by J.L. Curtis

- *The Way I Feel* by J. Cain

- *Why Am I Different?* by N. Simon & D. Leder

- *The Worst Day of My Life Ever* by J. Cook

Additional Resources

This section provides additional places to look for help and advice to develop your personal knowledge, as an adult, about this attribute.

Atlas of emotions. (n.d.). *The Ekmans' atlas of emotion*. Retrieved from http://atlasofemotions.org/

Bradberry, T., & Greaves, J. (2009). *Emotional Intelligence 2.0*. San Diego, CA: TalentSmart.

Cartwright, T. (2009). *Changing yourself and your reputation*. Greensboro, NC: Center for Creative Leadership.

Center for Creative Leadership. (2013). *Interpersonal savvy: Building and maintaining solid working relationships*. Greensboro, NC: Author.

Goldsmith, M., & Reiter, M. (2015). *Triggers: Creating behavior that lasts—becoming the person you want to be*. New York, NY: Crown Business.

Goleman, D. *Emotional intelligence*. (2005). New York, NY: Random House.

Kaplan, R. E., & Kaiser, R. B. (2013). *Fear your strengths: What you are best at could be your biggest problem*. San Francisco, CA: Berrett-Koehler Publishers.

King, S. N., & Altman, D. G. (2011). *Discovering the leader in you*. [Workbook]. San Francisco, CA: Jossey-Bass.

King, S. N., Altman, D. G., & Lee, R. J. (2011). *Discovering the leader in you: How to realize your leadership potential* (New and Rev. ed.). San Francisco, CA: Jossey-Bass.

Kirkland, K., & Manoogian, S. (1998). *Ongoing feedback: How to get it, how to use it.* Greensboro, NC: Center for Creative Leadership.

Mount, P., & Tardanico, S. (2014). *Beating the impostor syndrome.* Greensboro, NC: Center for Creative Leadership.

Philipson, P. J., & Gary, J. M. (2015). *Awareness in action: Self-awareness and group process.* Lanham, MD: University Press of America.

Rae, T. (2013). *Developing emotional literacy with teenagers: Building confidence, self-esteem and self- awareness.* London, England: SAGE.

Sternbergh, B., & Weitzel, S. R. (2001). *Setting your development goals.* Greensboro, NC: Center for Creative Leadership.

References

Hannum, K. M. (2007). Social identity: *Knowing yourself, leading others.* Greensboro, NC: Center for Creative Leadership.

Luft, J., & Ingham, H. (1955). The Johari Window, a graphic model of interpersonal awareness. Proceedings of the Western Training Laboratory in Group Development. Los Angeles, CA: UCLA.

"To me, accountable means that I have to be trustworthy and leading myself. Or, when you know that you did something wrong, you go and confess that you were the one because you know that was the right thing to do."

– Fourth Grade Student

Chapter 2
ACCOUNTABLE

•   •   •

"Being accountable to me means that you are responsible in remembering things and that you are honest about things."

– Seventh Grade Student

"Being accountable means establishing a reputation of being good to rely on; someone who does what they promise to do."

– Ninth Grade Student

Use the information in this section to help you introduce the "accountable" attribute to students. You can use the question stem "How does this attribute make you a better leader?" to start a discussion with your students and to check for comprehension (see the Additional Resources section in this chapter for more information to further your personal understanding).

Explaining "Accountable" to Students

We all make choices about how to act when we make mistakes. What do you do when you have made a mistake? How do you react when someone calls you out? Are you willing to admit when you are wrong? **Accountable means taking responsibility for your actions, even if there might be negative consequences.** Accountability means being willing to be vulnerable and courageous enough to admit the truth when you are in the wrong. By being willing to admit that you have made a mistake, you set an example for others, thus modelling strong leadership behavior.

What "Accountable" Looks Like

Self-aware leaders:

- recognize when they have made a mistake

- can be counted on to tell the truth regardless of the circumstances

- earn the trust and respect of others

- admit mistakes and avoid blaming others

- are transparent

- seek and accept feedback and put it to use

- are assertive and confident

- are secure enough to be vulnerable

- set a positive personal example by taking responsibility

- do not get defensive

- do not make excuses

- can admit when they have made mistakes

What Gets in the Way?

If you struggle with being accountable, you risk losing the trust of others; they might not believe they can count on you. If you are not willing to take responsibility for your actions, others may not want to work with you. Review the following list and note the items that might be keeping you from being accountable for your actions.

- You avoid admitting when you have made a mistake.

- You are unable to recognize when you are wrong.

- You are unwilling to accept feedback.

- You tend to blame your mistakes or shortcomings on others.

- You feel threatened when you make yourself vulnerable.

- You respond defensively when others notice a mistake you made.

- You let others accept responsibility for your mistakes.

- You overestimate what you are able to accomplish.

- You are not as forthcoming or honest with others as you could be.

- You make excuses and/or cover up your mistakes.

Being able to recognize and admit when you are wrong or have made a mistake can help you become a better and more trustworthy social-emotional leader.

Suggestions for Improving "Accountable" —————

Work with your students to discuss and establish some ways to build competency in this attribute. Below is a list to help support this exercise. Feel free to develop your own strategies or modify these suggestions.

You may also consider doing an activity with your students (see Activity Center in this chapter for suggestions) or asking them to write about the attribute (see Journal Prompts in this chapter for suggestions) to help build student understanding.

In conjunction with your students, figure out how you are going to support each other as a group or class to build competency in this leadership attribute.

- **Start small**. Think of a situation where you have not been accountable for your actions in the past. (For example, making an excuse for not completing your homework.) What could you have done differently?

- **Role play.** Practice with a partner what it is like to be accountable. (Example: "I'm sorry I didn't do my homework. I completely forgot it was due. Is there anything I can do to make it up?")

- **Consider the consequences.** What specifically can you gain when you take responsibility for your actions? What can you lose if you don't?

- **Seek feedback.** Ask a partner what they would do to take accountability in an uncomfortable situation.

- **Take action.** Being accountable isn't easy. It takes a certain amount of bravery. Dare to be courageous enough to admit when you're wrong. Do it!

- **Reflect and debrief.** Meet with your partner to discuss what happened when you were accountable.

Activity Center

Here are some suggestions for activities that may be modified to fit your context and the students with whom you are working.

- **Book introduction.** Find a book to read with students that has a character who either demonstrates accountability or who would have benefitted from being more accountable, and have students discuss or journal about the character's behavior (see the Suggested Books section of this chapter for books that could be used for this activity).

- **Accountability threats.** Ask students to identify reasons that can keep people from being accountable for their actions. Have them find a partner and discuss a situation in which they could have been more accountable for their actions, and what they could have done differently.

- **Accountability stories.** Have students think about a situation (fictional or real) where a choice has to be made about being accountable or not. Write two stories (or comic strips, videos, plays, etc.), one in which the character takes responsibility for their actions, and one in which the character does not. In each story, focus on the impact of this decision.

- **Accountability in the news.** Have students find a newspaper or journal article (online or print) in which a person does or does not demonstrate accountability. Share and discuss in small groups why they selected the article and the possible implications of the accountability choices described in the article.

- **Accountability in social media.** Have students reflect on ways to be accountable in various social media outlets. Have students give examples of how to be accountable for their actions on social media. Ask students for examples where social media detracts from accountability. Ask students to share and discuss in small groups how they can be more accountable in their online lives.

- **Noticing accountability.** For a specific amount of time (a few days, a week, two weeks) have students notice all the moments when accountability comes up. Have students capture these moments on their phones or by writing in a journal/notebook. Ask students to notice what was taking place and how they felt when it was happening. Have students discuss their findings in small or large groups. Ask them to look for themes from the situations or about how they felt. Ask students to reflect on the behaviors of the people in the situations: do they agree with the choices that were made, or do they think there are different choices that could have been made to demonstrate greater accountability?

Journal Prompts

Choose one or more of the journal prompts appropriate for the age level you work with. Feel free to modify or extend the prompt. Give students time to reflect on the questions in a personal journal. To extend the exercise, ask students to share their reflections with a peer or small group.

- Think of a situation in which you were not as accountable as you could have been. What led to that decision? What can you do to regain the other person' trust?

- Reflect on stories you have read. Describe a situation in which a character's accountability benefits themselves and/or others. How might you relate this situation to something in your life?

- Think of someone who is always accountable, regardless of the situation. What qualities set that person apart from others? How might you model some of those qualities?

- Have you ever been in a situation where someone else blamed you for something they should have been accountable for? What did it feel like? What do you wish the person would have done?

- Why might it be scary, or make you uncomfortable, to admit when you are wrong or have made a mistake?

Integrating the Attribute into Your Curriculum

Choose an activity from your planning guide or syllabus. After your students complete the activity, relate the activity back to the "accountable" attribute with a debriefing conversation. Below are suggested questions. Choose or modify questions based on your students' developmental level, your activity, and your context.

This debrief can take the form of a full-group discussion. You might consider giving students time to reflect on their answers with partners or in small groups before asking them to share responses with the larger group. Alternatively, you may decide to ask students to work in small groups to share their responses on flip charts, and then have a gallery walk where students walk around the room and read what other students have written, potentially adding their own comments or thoughts.

- How did the activity help you understand what "accountable" means?

- How did you work on being accountable during this activity?

- How did other students demonstrate being accountable during the activity?

- What does it mean to be accountable?

- Why is it important to be accountable?

- How can being accountable make you a better leader?

- How can a lack of accountability impact leadership?

- How can accountability be developed?

- What are some ways you could practice being accountable in the future?

- How will you demonstrate being accountable in your interactions with others?

- What impact can increasing accountability have on you?

- Identify a person, past or present, who demonstrates being accountable. What specific actions demonstrate this person being accountable?

- Identify a book character who demonstrates being accountable. What specific actions of this character demonstrate being accountable?

Questions to Assess Understanding

Consider giving the following questions to students to determine if you need to spend more time explaining this attribute.

- What does it mean to be accountable? Give an example of someone you know who shows accountability. How does this person demonstrate accountability?

- What are three things you are going to work on in order to become more accountable?

Suggested Books to Introduce "Accountable"

The books listed below can be used to deepen younger students' understanding of the "accountable" attribute.

- *I Like Me!* by N. Carlson

- *The Berenstain Bears and the Blame Game* by S. Berenstain & J. Berenstain

- *But It's Not My Fault* by J. Cook

- *Can People Count on Me?* by R. Nelson

- *Do I Have To? Kids Talk About Responsibility* by N. Loewen

- *Dog in Charge* by K.L. Going

- *I Am Responsible!* by D. Parker

- *"I'll Do It!" Taking Responsibility* by B. Moses & M. Gordon

- *Peace Week in Miss Fox's Class* by E. Spinelli

- *Stanley and the Class Pet* by B. Saltzberg

Additional Resources

This section provides additional places to look for help and advice to develop your personal knowledge, as an adult, about this attribute.

Brown, C. B. (2010). *The gifts of imperfection: Let go of who you think you're supposed to be and embrace who you are.* Center City, MN: Hazelden.

Brown, C. B. (2012). *Daring greatly: How the courage to be vulnerable transforms the way we live, love, parent, and lead.* New York, NY: Gotham Books.

Galindo, L. (2009). *The 85% solution: How personal accountability guarantees success—no nonsense, no excuses.* San Francisco, CA: Jossey-Bass.

Klann, G. (2007). *Building character: Strengthening the heart of good leadership.* San Francisco, CA: Jossey-Bass.

Miller, J. G., & Miller, K. G. (2016). *Raising accountable kids: How to be an outstanding parent using the power of personal responsibility.* New York, NY: TarcherPerigee.

Palanski, M. E., Cullen, K. L., Gentry, W. A., & Nichols, C. M. (2014). *Virtuous* leadership: Exploring the effects of leader courage and behavioral integrity on leader performance and image. *Journal of Business Ethics, 132(2),* 297-310.

"Resilient means to bounce back from a setback such as a bad grade on a test, or not winning a game."

– Seventh Grade Student

Chapter 3
RESILIENT

● ● ●

"Being resilient means not letting life's obstacles and problems make you give up, but keep going even though it is hard."

– 11th Grade Student

Introduction

Explaining "Resilient" to Students

We all have to deal with pressure, stressful situations, and setbacks. How do you feel when you face tough challenges? How do you react if you are not successful at achieving an important goal? Do others see you as someone who doesn't give up? **Resilient means continuing to try even in the face of failure or adversity.** When you are resilient, you are able to adapt to change and learn from challenges. To be resilient, it's important to believe in your ability to learn and grow. If you are resilient, then you do not give up, and you keep going even though it might be hard. This helps you learn how to deal with different situations or change.

What "Resilient" Looks Like

Resilient leaders:

- keep working on something, even when it is challenging

- don't give up

- maintain their composure under stress

- tolerate ambiguity or uncertainty

- adapt readily to new situations

- handle mistakes or setbacks with poise and grace

- put failures into perspective and do not dwell on them

- seek out help and support from others

- enjoy learning

- learn from failure or mistakes

What Gets in the Way?

Without resilience, you will lose out on opportunities to learn from challenges or setbacks, which can limit your potential to grow and adapt in the future. Review the following list and note the items that might be keeping you from being resilient.

- You shut down when something doesn't come easily to you.

- You ruminate about setbacks, rather than reflecting on how to learn from them.

- You are unwilling to ask for help.

- You give up when things get challenging.

- You blame others when something goes wrong.

- You don't respond well to change.

- You think everything should come easily.

- You overreact to setbacks.

- Being able to appreciate challenges and setbacks as learning opportunities can help you become more resilient.

Suggestions for Improving "Resilient" ——————————

Work with your students to discuss and establish some ways to build competency in this attribute. Below is a list to help support this exercise. Feel free to develop your own strategies or modify these suggestions.

You may also consider doing an activity with your students (see the Activity Center section in this chapter for suggestions) or asking them to write about the attribute (see the Journal Prompts section in this chapter for suggestions) to help build student understanding.

In conjunction with your students, figure out how you are going to support each other as a group or class to build competency in this leadership attribute.

- **Recognize the signals of stress.** Learn to pay attention to your body's response to challenges or setbacks. What are your physiological responses? Do you feel your heart rate going up? Do you get hot? Do you clench your jaw? The sooner you recognize that your body is going into stress, the sooner you can do something to manage it.

- **Regroup.** When you face failures, think: What can I learn from this so that I can do better next time? Identify people or places you can look to for support.

- **Develop self-care rituals.** These can be as simple as taking a deep breath or silently counting to ten whenever you start to feel upset or stressed. These short breaks will not take long and can help you approach the problem with a clear mind.

- **Put setbacks in perspective.** Do not run away from mistakes and failures, but do not dwell on them either. Strive to get beyond the pain and disappointment and refocus on what you can learn from the experience and what you can apply to future potentially stressful circumstances.

- **Create a plan.** Create a plan to focus on improving your resilience. Share this plan with a trusted peer or mentor.

- **Develop a support system.** Seek and build a diverse group of people you can rely on in difficult times. Having social support can help you deal with stressful or challenging situations more effectively.

- **Become a continuous learner.** Learn new skills, gain new understanding, and apply those lessons during times of stress and change. Be open to learning new approaches and letting go of old behaviors and skills that do not work anymore.

Activity Center

Here are some suggestions for activities that may be modified to fit your context and the students with whom you are working.

- **Book introduction.** Find a book to read with students that has a character who either demonstrates the "resilient" attribute or who would have benefitted from being more resilient, and have students discuss or journal about the character's behavior (see the Suggested Books section of this chapter for books that could be used for this activity).

- **Resilience challenges.** Have students identify what can keep people from being resilient. Have them find a partner and discuss a situation in which they could have been more resilient and what they could have done differently.

- **Resilience stories.** Have students think about a situation (fictional or real) where a person displays resilience. Write two stories (or comic strips, videos, skits, plays, etc.), one in which the character acts resiliently and one in which the character does not. In each story, focus on the impact of these actions.

- **Mistakes are a gift.** Have students create a song, spoken word, poem, or rap titled: "Mistakes are a gift."

- **Assess resilience.** Take the "Resilience Assessment" below and discuss results with a partner. Make a plan of some resilience strategies to work on.

- **Resilience reflection.** Ask students to work with a partner to respond to the following: Think of a time when you were unstoppable. What was your mindset like? How did you feel? What were the results of your actions? How can you use what you learned during this experience the next time you are faced with a difficult challenge?

- **Failure bulletin board.** Build a culture that appreciates failure as an opportunity for learning by having a failure bulletin board in your classroom. On this board, students celebrate failures as indicators that they are taking risks and trying new things.

- **Resilience in action.** Have students identify a place in their life where they believe practicing more resilience would have a positive impact on their lives. (Examples: learning to play an instrument, playing a sport, improving their mindset about a challenging class, practicing getting constructive feedback, etc.) Have students practice the ways to develop resilience in their selected setting and journal about or discuss the results of their actions.

Resilience Assessment

Look over the items in this checklist and darken the circle that most closely matches your assessment of yourself in each of five areas of resilience. What does your list tell you about your degree of resilience? What strengths can you rely on during times of challenge or change? What areas should you develop to become more resilient? Use what you learn to create a development plan to help you strengthen your resilience.

Strength
(indicates a skill you can rely on in times of change)

Development Need
(indicates a skill you should develop to increase your resilience)

| Greatest strength | | | | | | Greatest need |

Acceptance of Change

○ ○ ○ ○ ○ ○ ○

I am comfortable with change. I see it as an opportunity to grow as a leader.

Change makes me uneasy. I don't like facing new challenges without having some kind of control over the situation.

Continuous Learning

○ ○ ○ ○ ○ ○ ○

Change provides a chance for me to learn new skills and test new ideas. I like to build on the lessons of the past—my successes and my disappointments.

I want to stick with what I know best and with the skills that got me to this point in my life. Other people expect that—it's part of who I am.

Self-Empowerment

○ ○ ○ ○ ○ ○ ○

I regularly assess my strengths. I keep my eye out for challenges that will be difficult for me, so that I can learn new skills.

I have enough on my hands with all the things I am being asked to do regularly. I don't have time to seek out new challenges.

Personal Networks

○ ○ ○ ○ ○ ○ ○

I really appreciate my family, my friends, and other important people in my life. There have been many times that those relationships have helped me learn or deal with stressful situations. I like to stay connected to those people who are close to me and take a personal interest in their lives.

I don't like sharing my weaknesses or failures with my friends, family members, or other people in my life. I like to appear strong and self-sufficient.

Reflection

○ ○ ○ ○ ○ ○ ○

I make time each day to reflect on my decisions and actions. I like to look back to see if there was another choice I could have made.

There are always so many things to do. It's like running ahead of an avalanche. I don't have time to sit back and daydream about where I am going and how I am getting there.

Adapted from Pulley, M. L., & Wakefield, M. (2001). *Building resiliency: How to thrive in times of change.* Greensboro, NC: Center for Creative Leadership.

Journal Prompts

Choose one or more of the journal prompts appropriate for the age level you work with. Feel free to modify or extend the prompt. Give students time to reflect on the questions in a personal journal. To extend the exercise, ask students to share their reflections with a peer or small group.

- Think of a situation in which you were not as resilient as you could have been. What did that prevent you from learning? How could you have responded differently?

- What healthy strategies could you use to cope with setbacks or challenges?

- Think of people you know who stay calm and collected during stressful situations or failures. What are their strategies?

- Reflect on stories that you have read. Describe a situation in which a character's resilience benefits them and/or others. How might you relate the situation to something in your life?

- Why might it make you uncomfortable to ask for help when you've made a mistake? What support do you need to overcome your discomfort?

- What is the cost of not being resilient? What are the benefits of being resilient?

Integrating the Attribute into Your Curriculum

Choose an activity from your planning guide or syllabus. After your students complete the activity, relate the activity back to the "resilient" attribute with a debriefing conversation. Below are suggested questions. Choose or modify questions based on your students' developmental level, your activity, and your context.

This debrief can take the form of a full-group discussion. You might consider giving students time to reflect on their answers with partners or in small groups before asking them to share responses with the larger group. Alternatively, you may decide to ask students to work in small groups to share their responses on flip charts, and then have a gallery walk where students walk around the room and read what other students have written, potentially adding their own comments or thoughts.

- How did the activity help you understand the attribute "resilient"?

- How did you work on being resilient during this activity?

- How did other students demonstrate being resilient during the activity?

- What does it mean to be resilient?

- Why is it important to be resilient?

- How can being resilient make you a better leader?

- How can a lack of being resilient impact leadership?

- How can being resilient be developed?

- What are some ways you could practice being resilient moving forward?

- How will you demonstrate being resilient in your interactions with others?

- What impact can increasing resiliency have on you?

- Identify a person, past or present, who demonstrates being resilient. What specific actions demonstrate this person being resilient?

- Identify a book character who demonstrates being resilient. What specific actions of this character demonstrate being resilient?

Questions to Assess Understanding

Consider giving the following questions to students to determine if you need to spend more time explaining this attribute.

- What does it mean to be resilient? Give an example of someone you know who is resilient. How does this person demonstrate being resilient?

- What are three things you are going to work on in order to become more resilient?

Suggested Books to Introduce "Resilient" ———

The books listed below can be used to deepen younger students' understanding of the "resilient" attribute.

- *I Like Me!* by N. Carlson

- *After the Fall: How Humpty Dumpty Got Back Up Again: A Story* by D. Santat

- *Alexander and the Terrible, Horrible, No Good, Very Bad Day* by J. Viorst

- *Brave Irene* by W. Steig

- *Everyone Can Learn to Ride a Bicycle* by C. Raschka

- *The Most Magnificent Thing* by A. Spires

- *Nothing You Can't Do! The Secret Power of Growth Mindsets* by M.C. Ricci

- *Sam and Dave Dig a Hole* by M. Barnett

- *Stories of Persistence* by J. Colby

- *Whistle for Willie* by E.J. Keats

Additional Resources

This section provides additional places to look for help and advice to develop your personal knowledge, as an adult, about this attribute.

Brock, A., & Hundley, H. (2016). *The growth mindset coach: A teacher's month-by-month handbook for empowering students to achieve.* Berkeley, CA: Ulysses Press.

Clerkin, C., & Ronayne. P. (n.d.). *Resilience isn't futile: How brain-science can help us thrive in increasingly complex work environments* [Webinar]. Retrieved from http://insights.ccl.org/webinars/resilience-isnt-futile-how-brain-science-can-help-us-thrive-in-increasingly-complex-work-environments

Duckworth, A. (2016). *Grit: The power of passion and perseverance.* New York, NY: Scribner.

Greitens, E. (2016). *Resilience: Hard-won wisdom for living a better life*. Boston, MA: Houghton Mifflin Harcourt.

Hildrew, C. (2018). *Becoming a growth mindset school: The power of mindset to transform teaching, leadership, and learning*. New York, NY: Routledge.

Lama, D., & Tutu, D. (2016). *The book of joy: Lasting happiness in a changing world*. New York, NY: Avery.

Roger, D., & Petrie, N. (2016). *Work without stress: Building a resilient mindset for lasting success*. New York, NY: McGraw-Hill.

Ruderman, M. N., Braddy, P. W., Hannum, K. M., & Kossek, E. E. (2013). *Managing your whole life*. Greensboro, NC: Center for Creative Leadership.

Sanguras, L. Y. (2017). *Grit in the classroom: Building perseverance for excellence in today's students*. Waco, TX: Prufrock Press.

Seligman, M. E. (2006). *Learned optimism: How to change your mind and your life*. New York, NY: Vintage.

Seligman, M. E. (2007). *The optimistic child: A proven program to safeguard children against depression and build lifelong resilience*. New York, NY: Houghton Mifflin Harcourt.

Zolli, A., & Healy, A. M. (2012). *Resilience: Why things bounce back*. New York, NY: Free Press.

References

Pulley, M. L., & Wakefield, M. (2001). *Building resiliency: How to thrive in times of change*. Greensboro, NC: Center for Creative Leadership.

"In my grade, leadership looks like doing the right thing, not necessarily by being bold. It is easy for people to go with the grain, like making bad decisions such as drinking or even things like slacking in school. Leading in my grade means having discipline and staying true to values."

– 12th Grade Student

Chapter 4
INTEGRITY

• • •

"[Integrity] means that I am doing the right thing if someone is looking or not. I do what the person in charge says the first time, not the second time or more. It also means that I am listening and being aware of what the person is saying or doing. I do what the right thing is no matter if everybody else in the room is not doing the right thing. I make sure I take home the right supplies and turn work in on the correct due date."

– Fifth Grade Student

Introduction

Use the information in this section to help you introduce the "integrity" attribute to students. You can use the question stem "How does this attribute make you a better leader?" to start a discussion with your students and to check for comprehension (see the Additional Resources section in this chapter for more information to further your understanding).

Explaining "Integrity" to Students

We all have morals and values that guide how we act. Morals are shared beliefs within a community or society about what is right and wrong. What are some examples of right and wrong behavior? Values are your personal beliefs about what is most important to you. For example, family, kindness, and honesty. What are some of your strongest values? Do you regularly act in a way that is true to your values? **Integrity means acting in a way that is consistent with your values ("walking the talk") and demonstrates strong morals.** Acting with integrity can help you strengthen your relationships and build trust with other people, because you come across as honest and you act consistently in a way that is true to your personal values. To behave with integrity, it's important to understand both the morals and values that motivate you. If you act with integrity, other people will trust you and will be more willing to spend time with you and collaborate with you.

What "Integrity" Looks Like

Leaders who act with integrity:

- tell the truth (are honest)

- earn the trust and respect of others

- maintain confidentiality

- "walk the talk"—consistently match actions and words

- admit mistakes

- are transparent

- follow through on promises or commitments

- have a well-articulated set of morals and values

What Gets in the Way?

Individuals with integrity act in ways that build long-term relationships and trust with others. If you lack integrity, you may find that others are reluctant to work with you, leading to conflict. People may lose faith in your ability to work well with others. Review the following list and note the items that might interfere with you acting with integrity.

- You don't do what you say you're going to do.

- You say one thing, but your actions do not reflect your words.

- Role models or peers in your life do not consistently show good morals.

- You do not show who you are or talk about what you care about.

- You tend to focus on your own interests first.

- You have broken promises in the past.

- You're afraid to be fully honest with others.

- You are overly rigid in following your values—you do not understand that people can have different values, or you believe your values are superior.

- You sacrifice too much to uphold promises and commitments.

Understanding the morals and values that drive you, and working to act with integrity, can help you become a better leader.

Suggestions for Improving "Integrity"

Work with your students to discuss and establish some ways to build competency in this attribute. Below is a list to help support this exercise. Feel free to develop your own strategies or modify these suggestions. You may also consider doing an activity with your students (see Activity Center in this chapter for suggestions) or asking them to write about the attribute (see Journal Prompts in this chapter for suggestions) to help build student understanding.

In conjunction with your students, figure out how you are going to support each other as a group or class to build competency in this leadership attribute.

- **Keep promises.** Be clear about what you promise people and keep your commitments. If you find yourself going back on a promise, explain the situation and adjust your commitment.

- **Admit your mistakes.** Denial and defensiveness can damage your integrity. Hold yourself accountable. Quickly own up to your mistakes, try to understand what went wrong (including asking others), and move forward.

- **Be yourself.** Genuine leadership inspires trust and goodwill. Bring your unique character and talents to the work at hand—don't just present what you think others want to see.

- **Invite feedback.** It can be difficult to recognize when your words and actions are inconsistent. Seek others' observations and perceptions of your actions to become aware of inconsistencies and make adjustments in order to act with more integrity.

- **Share your values and morals with others.** Have conversations about what you care about and why.

Activity Center

Here are some suggestions for activities that may be modified to fit your context and the students with whom you are working.

- **Book introduction.** Find a book to read with students that has a character who either demonstrates "integrity" or who would have benefitted from having more integrity, and have students discuss or journal about the character's behavior (see the Suggested Books section of this chapter for books that could be used for this activity).

- **Define your values.** Have students work individually to list and define the values that are most important to them. (They can access a free online tool to help identify their personal values at https://www.valueableleaderproject.com/.) Optional follow-up: Have students share their values lists with a partner.

- **Integrity story.** Have students write a short story about someone acting with integrity.

- **Monologue or poem.** Have students write a poem or a monologue titled: "How I Show Integrity." Option: Share with the class.

- **Integrity survey.** Ask students to complete the Integrity Survey activity (p. 58).

- **Integrity project.** Have students research a historical figure who they think lived and acted with integrity. What challenges did that person face? What actions did they take that illustrate integrity? Were there times that person did not "walk the talk"? Was there a specific time in that person's life when they decided to live with integrity no matter what? Have students present their research in small groups or to the class.

- **Values skit.** Have students work in small groups to create short skits that demonstrate a value in action. Have the rest of the group guess which value is being demonstrated.

Integrity Survey

Complete this short survey. Then give it to at least five others (e.g., peers, teacher, parents) and ask them to rate you from 1, indicating you never do this, to 5, indicating you always do this.

My words and actions match.	1	2	3	4	5
I act in ways that support the morals of our school.	1	2	3	4	5
When having difficulty with another student, I go directly to them to discuss the problem.	1	2	3	4	5
I don't gossip about people behind their back.	1	2	3	4	5
Others can talk to me about their problems, knowing I will not share their secrets.	1	2	3	4	5
I am honest and straightforward.	1	2	3	4	5
My values are reflected in how I act.	1	2	3	4	5
I listen carefully to others.	1	2	3	4	5
I share my own opinions and perspectives, even when they are different from what others may think.	1	2	3	4	5
I take responsibility for my actions and the results of those actions.	1	2	3	4	5
I avoid blaming others; instead I focus on what can be done to fix the situation.	1	2	3	4	5

Once you receive your feedback, compare it to how you rated yourself. In a journal, answer the following question: What can I improve? Ask a trusted friend for suggestions about how to make adjustments. How will you make those improvements?

Journal Prompts

Choose one or more of the journal prompts appropriate for the age level you work with. Feel free to modify or extend the prompt. Give students time to reflect on the questions in a personal journal. To extend the exercise, ask students to share their reflections with a peer or small group.

- Do you make unrealistic promises? How can you make promises you are confident you can keep?

- If you have lost someone's trust, what events might have led to that? What can you do to regain their trust?

- What do you value most?

- What values drive your actions?

- What do your actions say about what you value? Are you aware of any inconsistencies?

- In what situations have you purposely not been direct or transparent in talking to others? What was your reasoning? What were the outcomes? How might the outcomes have been different if you had been more direct and transparent?

- How much of the "real you" do you show others? Should you show yourself more or less?

- Think of someone who is always authentic, regardless of the situation. What qualities set that person apart from others? How might you model some of those qualities?

- Choose one of the following quotes about integrity and describe a time when you, or someone you know, demonstrated this quote in real life:

  » "Real integrity is doing the right thing, knowing that nobody is going to know whether you did it or not." – Oprah Winfrey

» "The greatness of a man is not in how much wealth he acquires, but in his integrity and his ability to affect those around him positively." – Bob Marley

» "Keep true, never be ashamed of doing right, decide on what you think is right and stick to it." – George Eliot

Integrating the Attribute into Your Curriculum

Choose an activity from your planning guide or syllabus. After your students complete the activity, relate the activity back to the "integrity" attribute with a debriefing conversation. Below are suggested questions. Choose or modify questions based on your students' developmental level, your activity, and your context.

This debrief can take the form of a full-group discussion. You might consider giving students time to reflect on their answers with partners or in small groups before asking them to share responses with the larger group. Alternatively, you may decide to ask students to work in small groups to share their responses on flip charts, and then have a gallery walk where students walk around the room and read what other students have written, potentially adding their own comments or thoughts.

- How did the activity help you understand the attribute "integrity"?

- How did you work on integrity during this activity?

- How did other students demonstrate integrity during the activity?

- What does it mean to have integrity?

- Why is it important to have integrity?

- How can having integrity make you a better leader?

- How can a lack of integrity impact leadership?

- How can integrity be developed?

- What are some ways you could practice showing integrity moving forward?

- How will you demonstrate integrity in your interactions with others?

- How can acting with integrity benefit you?

- Identify a person, past or present, who demonstrates integrity. What specific actions demonstrate this person's integrity?

- Identify a book character who demonstrates integrity. What specific actions of this character demonstrate integrity?

Questions to Assess Understanding

Consider giving the following questions to students to determine if you need to spend more time explaining this attribute.

- What does it mean to have integrity? Give an example of someone you know who shows integrity. How does this person demonstrate integrity?

- What are three things you are going to work on in order to act with integrity?

Suggested Books to Introduce "Integrity"

The books listed below can be used to deepen younger students' understanding of the "integrity" attribute.

- *A Hen for Izzy Pippik* by A. Davis & M. Lafrance

- *The Empty Pot* by Demi

- *Purplicious* by E. Kann

- *Ruthie and the (Not So) Teeny Tiny Lie* by L. Rankin

- *Sam, Bangs & Moonshine* by E. Ness

- *Tell the Truth, B.B. Wolf* by J. Sierra & J. Seibold

Additional Resources

This section provides additional places to look for help and advice to develop your personal knowledge, as an adult, about this attribute.

Covey, S. M. R. (2006). *The speed of trust: The one thing that changes everything.* New York, NY: Free Press.

Criswell, C., & Campbell, D. (2008). *Building an authentic leadership image.* Greensboro, NC: Center for Creative Leadership.

Evans, C. (2015). *Leadership trust: Build it, keep it.* Greensboro, NC: Center for Creative Leadership.

Hernez-Broome, G., McLaughlin, C., & Trovas, S. (2006). *Selling yourself without selling out: A leader's guide to ethical self-promotion.* Greensboro, NC: Center for Creative Leadership.

Horsager, D. (2012). *The trust edge: How top leaders gain faster results, deeper relationships, and a stronger bottom line.* New York, NY: Free Press.

Horth, D. M., Miller, L., & Mount, P. (2016). *Leadership brand: Deliver on your promise.* Greensboro, NC: Center for Creative Leadership.

Stuecker, R. (2004). *Cultivating kindness in school: Activities that promote integrity, respect, and compassion in elementary and middle school students.* Champaign, IL: Research Press.

Stuecker, R. (2010). *Inspiring leadership in teens: Group activities to foster integrity, responsibility, and compassion.* Champaign, IL: Research Press.

LEADING WITH OTHERS

We live in a collaborative world. In order to lead with others, we need to be able to share responsibilities and recognize that everyone has something to contribute. This section includes information about the following leadership attributes:

ATTRIBUTES	DEFINITIONS
Collaborative	cooperates with others effectively
Communicative	expresses ideas clearly and effectively
Active Listener	listens carefully to what others have to say
Considerate	thinks about how their actions make other people feel
Respectful	treats other people the way they want to be treated
Accepting	appreciates the views of others, even if they are different from their own

"Leading with others means always including and thinking about others never just yourself; everyone is important, and you don't have to be the one in charge and shouldering everything—we can all work together."

– High School Student

Chapter 5
COLLABORATIVE

•   •   •

"Collaborative means to me that you work with others to become a team. I think that when you are collaborating that means to share ideas, use other peers ideas and come up with one big idea to do together."
– Fifth Grade Student

"Being able to work well with others is very important. Listening to their ideas and finding what works best for a situation will make it have the best possible outcome."
– Eighth Grade Student

Introduction

Explaining "Collaborative" to Students

No matter how much we may want to, we can't do everything alone. Research shows that collaboration between people who have different strengths or perspectives can result in better ideas and outcomes (Lazonder, 2005). How much time do you spend working with other people? How often are you willing to take others' ideas into consideration? How often do you combine your thoughts with thoughts of others to create new or better ideas? **Collaborative means being able to cooperate with others so that you can work together to achieve a shared goal.** In order to achieve a shared goal, there are three critical components that must be present: direction, alignment, and commitment (DAC) (McCauley & Fick-Cooper, 2015).

- **Direction** is agreement in the group about what it intends to accomplish.

- **Alignment** is coordinated work in the group.

- **Commitment** is the trust and mutual responsibility for the success and well-being of the group.

By being willing and able to work collaboratively with others, you will do better work and be able to achieve more.

What "Collaborative" Looks Like

Collaborative leaders:

- reach out to people and engage them in a common cause

- listen and are willing to be influenced

- quickly gain trust and respect from others

- address conflicts to support smooth, effective working relationships

- display emotional intelligence

- are good/active listeners

- care about people

- are seen as open and nonjudgmental

- put people at ease

- display warmth

- try to understand what other people think before making judgments

- seek common ground in an effort to build relationships

- seek first to understand others before being understood by them

- help or advocate for other people

- are able to work with others to agree on the outcomes of group work and how they are going to achieve these outcomes

What Gets in the Way?

People who struggle to collaborate with others can become isolated or excluded from important partnerships as peers lose interest in working with them. They are less likely to be trusted, which prevents the honest collaboration needed for success. Review the following list and note the items that might be keeping you from collaborating effectively with others.

- You're unwilling to listen to other people's thoughts and ideas.

- You're stubborn.

- You're not interested in what others want—only what you are after.

- You focus more on the task than the people.

- You don't trust other people.

- Your words don't match your actions. For example, you say that you are interested in other's ideas, but you interrupt them when they are speaking and don't listen to what they have to say.

- You do not think that other people's ideas are valuable.

- You're unwilling to integrate multiple ideas to create new ideas.

- You're unable to work with others to agree on a shared direction.

Being able to listen to and build upon other's thoughts, in order to support the collective needs of the group, and being able to work collaboratively on direction, alignment, and commitment, makes you a stronger leader.

Suggestions for Improving "Collaborative"

Work with your students to discuss and establish some ways to build competency in this attribute. Below is a list to help support this exercise. Feel free to develop your own strategies or modify these suggestions.

You may also consider doing an activity with your students (see the Activity Center section in this chapter for suggestions) or asking them to write about the attribute (see the Journal Prompts section in this chapter for suggestions) to help build student understanding.

In conjunction with your students, figure out how you are going to support each other as a group or class to build competency in this leadership attribute.

- **Listen actively.** Give people the opportunity to share their thoughts without any interruptions.

- **Think about your nonverbal communication.** People don't only listen to the words you say, but they also react to your facial expressions and body language. Focus on facial expressions and body language that invites collaboration. (Examples could include leaning in, nodding while someone is talking, smiling, etc.)

- **Focus on Yes, and...** If your default response to requests is "No" or "Yes, but..." try instead to respond with "Yes, and..." Focus on adding to ideas rather than shutting them down.

- **Ask others for their opinions, perspectives, and ideas.** Ask questions and show you are listening. Demonstrate you care about what others think.

- **Be open to other perspectives.** Look for opportunities to expand your way of thinking.

- **Be respectful.** Appreciate the diverse perspectives people bring to the table and try not to judge them when they are different from your own way of thinking (see chapter 10 for more information about accepting others).

- **Spend time with others.** Build trust by letting people get to know you better. Be kind and generous. Communicate clearly and openly. Above all, be sincere in your communication with others.

- **Work on DAC.** When working in groups, make sure that everyone in the group understands and agrees on the goals of the work (direction), how the work will be accomplished (alignment), and how they will put the goals of the group first (commitment).

Activity Center

Here are some suggestions for activities that may be modified to fit your context and the students with whom you are working.

- **Book introduction.** Find a book to read with students that has a character who either demonstrates the "collaborative" attribute or who would have benefitted from being more collaborative, and have students discuss or journal about the character's behavior (see the Suggested Books section of this chapter for books that could be used for this activity).

- **DAC Boat exercise.** Put students in groups of four to five.

  » Ask students to stand in a line with their group, close their eyes, and face their body toward the direction that they believe is north. Ask students to keep their eyes closed and imagine that they are in a boat and a huge storm is coming toward them. In order to escape the storm they must start paddling north, toward the shore. Ask them to move their arms like they are rowing.

  » Ask them to open their eyes while they are still paddling. Have students take a few minutes to communicate with their group about what they need to do in order to successfully reach the shore. Have each group demonstrate how it will get to shore and get feedback from other groups (this will go faster as each group goes as they will learn from each other).

  » Have a discussion with the whole group about DAC and relate it to the different roles people took. Ask about how they decided on **direction** (How did they reach consensus about the direction they were facing? Was everyone clear on the goal?), **alignment** (How did they coordinate their rowing or paddling? Was there a navigator or coxswain? What happens if they all paddle on the same side? How was the rhythm established?), and **commitment** (How much effort did each person put in to achieve the group's goal of reaching shore? What if only one person was rowing?). How does this brief experience help us understand the importance of collaboration?

- **Activities for building DAC for workgroups.** Before starting group work, have groups collectively fill out the Building DAC worksheet that follows this section on p. 74.

- **Paper towers.** Have students work in small groups of four to five students to build the tallest free-standing tower, using only newspaper and tape. Also ask them to work together to name and create a nameplate for their tower. Provide about 10 minutes for the building. Have groups present their tower and describe how they collaborated to create and build it. Have groups discuss how DAC showed up in this activity.

- **Combining ideas.** Pose a problem-solving question. (Examples: What is one thing you could do to make your school a better place? How could you eliminate plastic waste?) Each student writes down an idea to answer the question, and these ideas are all put into a bowl or hat. Students then work in groups of three to four, and each person within the group selects a random idea from the hat. The students must work together to combine the ideas to come up with one idea to share with the group. For an extra challenge: After each group has come up with an idea, combine two or more groups so that they have to work together to merge their ideas into one.

- **Yes, and...** activity. Have students choose a partner (or work in small groups of three to four).

  » *Round 1:* The first person starts by saying, "I have a great idea! Let's..." and the partner completes the sentence. The first person responds with "No, because..."

  » *Round 2:* The first person repeats the starting phrase: "I have a great idea! Let's..." and the partner responds with "Yes, but..."

  » *Round 3:* The first person repeats the starting phrase: "I have a great idea! Let's..." The other person responds with "Yes, and..." and builds on the idea by adding to it.

  » Have students discuss as a group what it feels like to hear each of those different responses.

Building DAC

Before starting to work on a project with a group, it is important to think about DAC. Fill out the following table as a group.

Direction	What are you trying to accomplish?	
	How will you know if you have been successful?	
Alignment	How are you going to accomplish your goals(s)?	
	Who is going to be responsible for what?	
	What is the timeframe for completing each part of the work?	
Commitment	How will you show that you are dedicated to achieving the group goal?	
	What agreements will you make as a group about how you are going to work together?	
	How will you hold each other accountable for meeting those agreements?	

Journal Prompts

Choose one or more of the journal prompts appropriate for the age level you work with. Feel free to modify or extend the prompt. Give students time to reflect on the questions in a personal journal. To extend the exercise, ask students to share their reflections with a peer or small group.

- What does an ideal collaborator look like? What are your strengths and challenges in collaborating with others? What can you do to become a better collaborator?

- Why is it important to establish group norms (the rules about what is acceptable or unacceptable during group work)? How do norms contribute to effective collaboration?

- Describe a group (in or out of school) you worked with where collaboration went well. Why did it work so well? Describe a group you worked with where collaboration failed. Why did it fail? What could the group have done differently to collaborate more effectively? What did DAC look like within the group?

- How do you think other people perceive you when you are working in groups? Do others perceive you as the person who talks all the time? Do others view you as the person who lets other people do the work? Do others experience you as the person who listens to all ideas and tries to combine them? How do you want to be seen by others as a collaborator?

- Why is collaboration important? What are some real-life situations where collaboration is necessary?

- Think about someone you have observed (in real life or in a movie or television show) who is a great collaborator. What makes this person a great collaborator?

Integrating the Attribute into Your Curriculum

Choose an activity from your planning guide or syllabus. After your students complete the activity, relate the activity back to the "collaborative" attribute with a debriefing conversation. Below are suggested questions. Choose or modify questions based on your students' developmental level, your activity, and your context.

This debrief can take the form of a full-group discussion. You might consider giving students time to reflect on their answers with partners or in small groups before asking them to share responses with the larger group. Alternatively, you may decide to ask students to work in small groups to share their responses on flip charts, and then have a gallery walk where students walk around the room and read what other students have written, potentially adding their own comments or thoughts.

- How did the activity help you understand the attribute "collaborative"?

- How did you work on being collaborative during this activity?

- How did other students demonstrate being collaborative during the activity?

- What does it mean to be collaborative?

- Why is it important to be collaborative?

- How can being collaborative make you a better leader?

- How can a lack of being collaborative impact leadership?

- How can you develop your ability to be collaborative?

- What are some ways you could practice being collaborative in the future?

- How will you demonstrate being collaborative in your interactions with others?

- What impact can increasing your ability to be collaborative have on you?

- Identify a person, past or present, who demonstrates being collaborative. What specific actions does this person take that demonstrate being collaborative?

- Identify a book character who demonstrates being collaborative. What specific actions does this character take that demonstrate being collaborative?

Questions to Assess Understanding

Consider giving the following questions to students to determine if you need to spend more time explaining this attribute.

- What does it mean to be collaborative? Give an example of someone you know who is collaborative. How does this person demonstrate being collaborative?

- Explain the DAC model. How is DAC related to collaboration?

- What are three things you are going to work on in order to become more collaborative?

Suggested Books to Introduce "Collaborative" ────────────

The books listed below can be used to deepen younger students' understanding of the "collaborative" attribute.

- *The Crayon Box that Talked* by S. DeRolf & M. Letzig

- *How To Make Decisions as a Group* by J. Turner

- *Pitch In! Kids Talk About Cooperation* by P.H. Nettleton & A.B. Muehlenhardt

- *Sam and Dave Dig a Hole* by M. Barnett

- *Swimmy* by L. Lionni

- *The Wolf, the Duck and the Mouse* by M. Barnett & J. Klassen

Additional Resources

This section provides additional places to look for help and advice to develop your personal knowledge, as an adult, about this attribute.

Aronson, E., & Patnoe, S. (2011). *Cooperation in the classroom: The jigsaw method.* London, England: Printer & Martin.

Bordessa, K. (2005). *Team challenges: 170+ group activities to build cooperation, communication, and creativity.* Chicago, IL: Zephyr Press.

Center for Creative Leadership. (2007). *Leadership Networking: Connect, Collaborate, Create* [Webinar]. Greensboro, NC: Author.

Center for Creative Leadership. (2013). *Interpersonal savvy: Building and maintaining solid working relationships.* Greensboro, NC: Author.

Goleman, D. (1998). *Working with emotional intelligence.* New York, NY: Bantam Books.

Goleman, D. (2006). *Emotional intelligence.* New York, NY: Bantam Books.

Goleman, D. (2011). *Leadership: The power of emotional intelligence.* Northampton, MA: More Than Sound.

Stone, E. (2017). The science behind the growing importance of collaboration. *Kellogg Insight.* Retrieved from https://insight.kellogg.northwestern.edu/article/the-science-behind-the-growing-importance-of-collaboration

Klann, G. (2004). *Building your team's morale, pride, and spirit.* Greensboro, NC: Center for Creative Leadership.

Kram, K. E., & Ting, S. (2006). Coaching for emotional competence. In: S. Ting & P. Scisco (Eds.), *The CCL handbook of coaching: A guide for the leader coach* (pp. 179–202). San Francisco, CA: Jossey-Bass.

Maxwell, J. C. (2004). *Relationships 101: What every leader needs to know.* Nashville, TN: Thomas Nelson Publishers.

Sobel, A., & Panas, J. (2012). *Power questions: Build relationships, win new business, and influence others.* Hoboken, N.J: Wiley.

Steltzner, A. (2016). *The right kind of crazy: A true story of teamwork, leadership, and high-stakes innovation.* New York, NY: Portfolio/Penguin.

References

Lazonder, A. W. (2005). Do two heads search better than one? Effects of student collaboration on web search behaviour and search outcomes. *British Journal of Educational Technology, 36*(3), 465–475.

McCauley, C., & Fick-Cooper, L. (2019). *Direction, alignment, commitment: Achieving better results through leadership (2nd ed.).* Greensboro, NC: Center for Creative Leadership.

"Communicative means listen to each other and know what they mean and what they are saying. And help explain what they're saying."

– Third Grade Student

Chapter 6
COMMUNICATIVE

• • •

"[Being communicative means] to tell people what you are thinking and how we can do better as a unit to accomplish a similar goal."
– Seventh Grade Student

"Being communicative means that you can communicate and express your and other's ideas in a respectable way."
– 11th Grade Student

Introduction

Use the information in this section to help you introduce the "communicative" attribute to students. You can use the question stem "How does this attribute make you a better leader?" to start a discussion with your students and to check for comprehension (see the Additional Resources section in this chapter for more information to further your personal understanding).

Explaining "Communicative" to Students

The greatest challenge for any leader is to communicate effectively. How well can you talk about your ideas clearly and concisely? Can you listen objectively to others' ideas? Can you adapt your communication style based on the situation you're in? **Skill in being communicative means being able to express your ideas and the ideas of others clearly and effectively.** To develop this important leadership attribute, you need to be able to articulate your own ideas clearly, be open to hearing others' ideas and perspectives, show respect for others' ideas, and be able to help others articulate their ideas. Good communicators speak, write, and listen, clearly and consistently. By being able to express your ideas and the ideas of others clearly and effectively, you will help your group be more successful.

What "Communicative" Looks Like

Leaders who communicate well:

- are crisp, clear, and articulate

- adapt their communications based on others' needs

- listen carefully to others' ideas and suggestions

- can effectively convey a message in speech or in writing

- make group goals and plans clear

- encourage others to share their ideas

- are forthright in expressing themselves

- practice active listening

- help or advocate for other people

What Gets in the Way?

Communicating is a highly visible skill. It is readily apparent when leaders can't present ideas clearly to others. If you are not ensuring that all voices are heard and understood, members of the group may feel alienated, and the group won't function well. Review the following list and note the items that might be keeping you from being an effective communicator.

- You have not developed active listening skills.

- You're unwilling to listen to other people's thoughts and ideas.

- You don't understand the specific needs and interests of your audience.

- You're not able to adapt your communication style.

- You don't share your ideas because you worry that they will be criticized.

- You don't encourage others to share their ideas.

- You overwhelm people with details they don't need to know.

- You focus so much on listening to others that you don't express your own opinion enough.

- You focus so much on your idea that you don't try to understand others' ideas.

- You don't take the time to help explain others' ideas to everyone.

Poor communication within a group leads to less effective outcomes. Being able to communicate your ideas clearly and encouraging everyone to listen to and understand each other's ideas will help you become a better leader.

Suggestions for Improving "Communicative"

Work with your students to discuss and establish some ways to build competency in this attribute. Below is a list to help support your efforts. Feel free to develop your own strategies or modify these suggestions.

You may also consider doing an activity with your students (see this chapter's Activity Center for suggestions) or asking them to write about the attribute (see Journal Prompts for suggestions) to help build student understanding.

In conjunction with your students, figure out how you are going to support each other as a group or class to build competency in this leadership attribute.

- **Listen to other perspectives first.** Before offering your own ideas and perspectives, take a moment to ask others about their thoughts and their point of view. This will help you understand what others are thinking and help you communicate your own ideas more effectively. This is especially important when dealing with complex situations where there might be many different perspectives.

- **Be an active listener.** People who listen are listened to. Active listening strategies such as paying attention, listening without judging, reflecting, clarifying, summarizing, sharing, and reading nonverbal cues can all be practiced and improved.

- **Check for understanding.** Summarize what others have said and ask them if this summary correctly reflects what they were trying to say.

- **Record yourself.** Video yourself talking with others and watch it. What emotions did you see yourself convey? Does your body language match your speech?

- **Tell stories tied to your point.** Giving examples through brief, relevant stories creates more effective and engaging communication. For example, sharing a story about how a problem was solved helps your listeners see themselves in your story. Make sure that the story relates to the point of the message you are trying to convey.

- **Be straightforward.** Be open, honest, and straightforward when you communicate. Make sure people understand what you are trying to say.

- **Know your audience.** Be aware of who you are talking to and their level of understanding. Think about how to adjust your vocabulary and the amount of background knowledge you need to give.

- **Learn from the best.** Find a role model—in real life, the movies, or social media—who communicates really well. Reflect on what this person does that makes them such an effective communicator. Use this person's strategies as a model for your own communication.

- **Practice!** Think about what you are going to say. Write it down. Practice it with a peer or mentor. Rewrite and practice again!

Activity Center

Here are some suggestions for activities that may be modified to fit your context and the students with whom you are working.

- **Book introduction.** Find a book to read with students that has a character who either demonstrates the attribute "communicative" or who would have benefitted from being more communicative, and have students discuss or journal about the character's behavior (see the Suggested Books section of this chapter for books that could be used for this activity).

- **So what I hear you say is...** In groups of three, one student tells a story or gives a presentation. The second person communicates their understanding of what the first person said, starting with, "So what I hear you say is..." Then the third person, who just observes for the other two, evaluates this summary and gives feedback about the effectiveness of the summary at communicating the intended information, whether they think there was something missing from the summary, or whether there were things the presenter could have done better to communicate their point. Then ask students to switch roles.

- **Communicators in the media.** Have students work in small groups to select someone in the media who is a good communicator and someone who is a bad communicator. Compare and contrast the good and the bad communicator. Have students present their findings to another group or to the whole class.

- **Book tweets.** Have students summarize a famous speech or a chapter in a book they're reading with a tweet (280 characters that summarize the essence of the original text).

- **Effective communicator.** Ask students to find a short video clip of someone they would describe as an effective communicator. Have them show the clip to the class and explain why they selected it.

- **Communication across audiences.** Have students work in small groups (four to five people) to create a presentation about how to communicate effectively: one for six year olds, one for their peers, and one for their parents or teachers. Have them think about the following questions: What is different about how you communicate to each of those groups? How can this help you when you be more aware of how you communicate with others?

Journal Prompts

Choose one or more of the journal prompts appropriate for the age level you work with. Feel free to modify or extend the prompt. Give students time to reflect on the questions in a personal journal. To extend the exercise, ask students to share their reflections with a peer or small group.

- What does a good communicator look like? What are your strengths and challenges in communicating with others? What can you do to get better at communicating with others?

- Think about someone you have observed (in real life) who is a great communicator. What makes this person a great communicator?

- List some steps you can take to make sure all voices are heard when you are working with a group. Which of these steps do you do already? Which could you do better?

- How do you know when you're communicating effectively? What does it feel like? What do you notice about the people with whom you are communicating?

- Choose something in the room and try to describe it without writing what it is. Try to challenge yourself to choose something difficult. *For a bonus activity: Share this description with a partner and see if they can guess what it is.*

Integrating the Attribute into Your Curriculum ──────────

Choose an activity from your planning guide or syllabus. After your students complete the activity, relate the activity back to the "communicative" attribute with a debriefing conversation. Below are suggested questions. Choose or modify questions based on your students' developmental level, your activity, and your context.

You might consider giving students time to reflect on their answers with partners or in small groups before asking them to share responses with the larger group. Alternatively, you may decide to ask students to work in small groups to share their responses on flip charts, and then have a gallery walk where students walk around the room and read what other students have written, potentially adding their own comments or thoughts.

- How did the activity help you understand the attribute "communicative"?

- How did you work on being communicative during this activity?

- How did other students demonstrate being communicative during the activity?

- What does it mean to be communicative?

- Why is it important to be communicative?

- How can being communicative make you a better leader?

- How can a lack of being communicative impact leadership?

- How can you develop your ability to be more communicative?

- What are some ways you could practice being communicative moving forward?

- How will you demonstrate being communicative in your interactions with others?

- What impact can increasing your ability to be communicative have on you?

- Identify a person, past or present, who demonstrates being communicative. What specific actions demonstrate this person being communicative?

- Identify a book character who demonstrates being communicative. What specific actions of this character demonstrate being communicative?

Questions to Assess Understanding

Consider giving the following questions to students to determine if you need to spend more time explaining this attribute.

- What does it mean to be communicative? Give an example of someone you know who is a good communicator. How does this person demonstrate being communicative?

- What are three things you are going to work on in order to become more communicative?

Suggested Books to Introduce "Communicative"

The books listed below can be used to deepen younger students' understanding of the "communicative" attribute.

- *A Squiggly Story* by A. Larsen

- *Decibella and Her 6-Inch Voice* by J. Cook

- *My Mouth Is a Volcano!* by J. Cook

- *Sam and Dave Dig a Hole* by M. Barnett

Additional Resources to Further Understanding

This section provides additional places to look for help and advice to develop your personal knowledge, as an adult, about this attribute.

Bolton, R. (1986). *People skills: How to assert yourself, listen to others, and resolve conflicts.* New York, NY: Touchstone.

Center for Creative Leadership (2019). *Active listening: Improve your ability to listen and lead (2nd ed.).* Greensboro, NC: Center for Creative Leadership.

Fleming, C. A. (2013). *It's the way you say it: Becoming articulate, well-spoken, and clear.* San Francisco, CA: Berrett-Koehler.

Frey, N., Fisher, D., & Smith, D. (2019). *All learning is social and emotional: Helping students develop essential skills for the classroom and beyond.* Alexandria, VA: ASCD.

Maxwell, J. (2010). *Everyone communicates, few connect.* Nashville, TN: Thomas Nelson.

Patterson, K., Grenny, J., McMillan, R., and Switzler, A. (2011). *Crucial conversations. (2nd ed.).* New York, NY: McGraw Hill.

Prince, D.W., and Hoppe, M.H. (2000). *Communicating across cultures.* Greensboro, NC: Center for Creative Leadership.

Scharlatt, H., & Smith, R. (2014). *Influence: Gaining commitment, getting results (2nd ed.).* Greensboro, NC: Center for Creative Leadership.

Zweifel, T. D. (2003). *Communicate or die: Getting results through speaking and listening.* New York, NY: SelectBooks.

"[Active listeners] listen carefully to everyone's ideas or thoughts even if you don't agree with them."

– Fourth Grade Student

Chapter 7
ACTIVE LISTENER

•   •   •

"Active listening means paying attention and asking clarifying
questions when necessary."
– 12th Grade Student

Introduction

Use the information in this section to help you introduce the "active listener" attribute to students. You can use the question stem "How does this attribute make you a better leader?" to start a discussion with your students and to check for comprehension (see Additional Resources for more information to further your personal understanding).

Explaining "Active Listener" to Students

The first step to becoming a great leader is being a great listener. How often do you connect with others by listening attentively? Do you ask questions in order to truly understand the other person's point of view? **Being an active listener means listening carefully to what others have to say.** Active listening includes paying attention, suspending judgment, reflecting, clarifying, summarizing, sharing, and reading nonverbal cues. Before you can lead with others, you need to understand what others are thinking and feeling. People who listen are listened to.

What "Active Listener" Looks Like

Leaders who are active listeners:

- understand others' needs, motivations, and points-of-view

- listen carefully to others' ideas and suggestions

- understand others' nonverbal communication

- use nonverbal communication to demonstrate listening (e.g., nodding in agreement, eye contact)

- pay attention when others are speaking

- listen without judgment

- reflect on what others are saying

- ask clarifying questions

- are able to summarize what they have heard

- are able to communicate their understanding of another person's ideas

What Gets in the Way?

Without active listening, people might feel you don't care about hearing them or understanding their point of view. You may miss out on opportunities to build strong relationships and connections with others if you are unable to be an active listener. You may also find that you are spending time arguing with someone who actually agrees with you. A lack of active listening can keep you from leading well with others. Review the following list and note the items that might be keeping you from being an active listener.

- You talk more than you listen.

- You judge what the person is saying.

- You make assumptions without clarification.

- You do not ask questions.

- You are thinking about what you want to say rather than listening carefully to what is being said.

- You do not pay attention to nonverbal cues.

- You do not take time to process what others have said before responding.

Being an active listener will help you understand other people's feelings and perspectives, which will make you a better social-emotional leader.

Suggestions for Improving "Active Listener"

Work with your students to discuss and establish some ways to build competency in this attribute. Below is a list to help support this exercise (Center for Creative Leadership, 2019). Feel free to develop your own strategies or modify these suggestions.

You may also consider doing an activity with your students (see Activity Center for suggestions) or asking them to write about the attribute (see Journal Prompts for suggestions) to help build student understanding.

In conjunction with your students, figure out how you are going to support each other as a group or class to build competency in this leadership attribute.

- **Pay attention.** One of the main goals of active listening is to set a comfortable tone and allow time for the other person to speak and think. In addition to paying attention to the speaker's verbal and nonverbal cues, make sure to pay attention to the following:

  » **Your frame of mind.** Be present and focused on the moment. Focus your intent on being the best listener and learner that you can be. This is not about you sharing your opinion. Remember that your intention is to understand and connect with the other person.

  » **Your body language.** Show interest in what the other person is saying. Make comfortable eye contact. Lean forward and keep an open body posture. Indicate understanding with appropriate reactions (e.g., head nods, smiles).

  » **Work on reading nonverbal cues.** Pay close attention to the speaker's nonverbal behavior to pick up on the important information it offers. Look for and pay attention to tone of voice, intensity, loudness, facial expressions, and posture to understand the emotions that underlie the perspective the person is sharing. Watch for shifts in body, language, and voice.

- **Suspend judgment.** Active listening requires an open mind. You do not need to agree with what the other person is saying, but you do need to try to understand their point of view before sharing your own. Be comfortable not talking and just listening. Here are some strategies you can use for suspending judgment: practice empathy (try to put yourself in the other person's shoes), indicate that you have an open mind (try saying "My goal here is to understand, not to judge"), acknowledge differences (try saying "I know we're looking at this situation in different ways, and I want to understand how you're looking at it"), and be patient (allow the other person to elaborate without trying to speed them along).

- **Reflect.** Think of yourself as a mirror and reflect the other person's information or emotions back to them without agreeing or disagreeing. Demonstrate that you are listening by regularly paraphrasing the information you are hearing. You can say, "What I'm hearing you say is..." or "Just to check my understanding, you are saying..." Also, work on paraphrasing the emotion you are hearing. For example, "It sounds to me like you're feeling pretty frustrated about..."

- **Clarify.** Check your understanding by asking questions. These questions can be:

  » open-ended—encourage people to expand on their ideas. (Example: "What are your thoughts on...")

  » clarifying—clear up confusion. (Example: "Let me see if I'm clear; are you talking about...?")

  » probing—highlight details and introduce new suggestions or ideas. (Example: "What is it in your own leadership approach that might be contributing to your group struggling with this project?")

- **Summarize.** Restate the core themes you are hearing the other person say in your own words. This helps the other person see their key points and shows that you were listening and that you understand their point of view. Summarizing what you hear does not imply you agree or disagree with what was said.

- **Share.** Active listening is about first understanding the other person and then sharing your thoughts, ideas, and perspective. After you understand the other person's perspective, you should work on sharing your view and relating it to what you heard them say. For example, "Your telling me about a student gossiping about you behind your back made me think about when a similar thing happened to my friend at a different school. Here's what they did..."

Activity Center

Here are some suggestions for activities that may be modified to fit your context and the students with whom you are working.

- **Book introduction.** Find a book to read with students that has a character who demonstrates the attribute "active listener" or who would have benefitted from being a better active listener, and have students discuss or journal about the character's behavior (see the Suggested Books section of this chapter for books that could be used for this activity).

- **"Active Listening" reflection.** Have students identify reasons that can keep people from being active listeners. With a peer, ask students to discuss a situation in which they could have listened more actively. What got in their way? What could they have done differently?

- **Practice active listening.** Put students into pairs. Have your partner talk for one minute about a favorite song, a favorite holiday, a favorite vacation, a favorite class, something they are passionate about, etc. (choose one). Ask students to listen for facts and then summarize these facts back to the person who shared. Then switch. For a more difficult task, have students explain to others what their partner communicated to them.

- **Active vs. non-active listening.** Put students into pairs. Have one person talk for one minute while the other person works to NOT actively listen. Then have the same person talk for another minute while the other person works to practice active listening skills. Then have the students switch roles. In the activity debrief, ask students to discuss the difference between the first two rounds. Ask students how they felt during each round and how the active versus non-active listening impacted their relationship with the other person.

- **Shared storytelling.** Going around the classroom, create a group story by having each student contribute one word at a time. Nobody can speak twice until every student has shared one word. Students have to pay attention to all the words others are saying to make a story that makes sense.

- **Back-to-back art.** Have students sit back-to-back with a partner. Give one student a fairly simple piece of art. The student with the artwork describes it, and the other student tries to draw what is described.

- **Nonverbal cues.** One aspect of active listening is paying attention to nonverbal cues. Write down a number of emotions on index cards (e.g., happy, sad, angry). Ask students to write a short story about a trip they took. Then have them select an index card and share their story while modelling the emotion on the index card. Then have them select a different card and share their story again, displaying a different emotion (the words of the story may not change). Have the rest of the students write down the emotion they believe the student is trying to share and why they think that. (This could be done as a small-group activity.)

Journal Prompts

Choose one or more of the journal prompts appropriate for the age level you work with. Feel free to modify or extend the prompt. Give students time to reflect on the questions in a personal journal. To extend the exercise, ask students to share their reflections with a peer or small group.

- Think of a time when someone did not actively listen to what you had to say. How did this make you feel?

- How does it make you feel when you can tell that someone understands you? Write about a situation where you felt deeply listened to and understood.

- Identify areas in which you could be a better active listener. Describe what you could do differently.

- Think about a time when someone's nonverbal cues (body language and facial expressions) didn't match what they were saying. What impact did that have on you as the listener? What are some clarifying questions you could have asked?

- Think about situations or times when it is difficult for you to listen actively. When is this most common, and what can you do to be a better active listener in these situations?

Integrating the Attribute into Your Curriculum

Choose an activity from your planning guide or syllabus. After your students complete the activity, relate the activity back to the "active listener" attribute with a debriefing conversation. Below are suggested questions. Choose or modify questions based on your students' developmental level, your activity, and your context.

This debrief can take the form of a full-group discussion. You might consider giving students time to reflect on their answers with partners or in small groups before asking them to share responses with the larger group. Alternatively, you may decide to ask students to work in small groups to share their responses on flip charts, and then have a gallery walk where students walk around the room and read what other students have written, potentially adding their own comments or thoughts.

- How did the activity help you understand the attribute "active listener"?

- How did you work on being an active listener during this activity?

- How did other students demonstrate active listening during the activity?

- What does it mean to be an active listener?

- Why is it important to be an active listener?

- How can being an active listener make you a better leader?

- How can not being an active listener impact leadership?

- How can you develop your ability to be an active listener?

- What are some ways you could practice active listening moving forward?

- How will you demonstrate being an active listener in your interactions with others?

- What impact can increasing your ability to be an active listener have on you?

- Identify a person, past or present, who demonstrates being an active listener. What specific actions demonstrate this person being an active listener?

- Identify a book character who demonstrates being an active listener. What specific actions of this character demonstrate being an active listener?

Questions to Assess Understanding

Consider giving the following questions to students to determine if you need to spend more time explaining this attribute.

- What does it mean to be an active listener? Give an example of someone you know who is an active listener. How does this person demonstrate active listening?

- What are three things you are going to work on in order to become a better active listener?

Suggested Books to Introduce "Active Listener"

The books listed below can be used to deepen younger students' understanding of the "active listener" attribute.

- *How Do We Listen?* by J. Laffin & T. Kügler

- *Howard B. Wigglebottom Learns to Listen* by H. Binkow

- *Interrupting Chicken* by D. E. Stein

- *My Mouth Is a Volcano!* by J. Cook

- *The Rabbit Listened* by C. Doerrfeld

- *Why Should I Listen?* by C. Llewellyn

- *The Worst Day of My Life Ever!* by J. Cook

Additional Resources to Further Understanding

This section provides additional places to look for help and advice to develop your personal knowledge, as an adult, about this attribute.

Bolton, R. (1986). *People skills: How to assert yourself, listen to others, and resolve conflicts.* New York, NY: Touchstone.

Cain, S. (2013). *Quiet: The power of introverts in a world that can't stop talking.* New York, NY: Broadway Books.

Center for Creative Leadership. *The big 6: An active listening skill set.* Retrieved from: https://www.ccl.org/multimedia/podcast/the-big-6-an-active-listening-skill-set/

Donoghue, P. J., & Siegel, M. E. (2005). *Are you really listening? Keys to successful communication.* Notre Dame, IN: Sorin Books.

Karas, S. (1998). *Changing the world one relationship at a time: Focused listening for mutual support & empowerment.* Freedom, CA: Crossing Press.

Maxwell, J. (2010). *Everyone communicates, few connect.* Nashville, TN: Thomas Nelson.

Nichols, M. P. (2009). *The lost art of listening: How learning to listen can improve relationships.* New York, NY: Guilford Press.

Patterson, K., Grenny, J., McMillan, R., & Switzler, A. (2011). *Crucial conversations. (2nd ed.).* New York, NY: McGraw Hill.

References

Center for Creative Leadership (2019). *Active listening: Improve your ability to listen and lead (2nd ed.).* Greensboro, NC: Center for Creative Leadership.

*"Considerate means to me
thinking about the way I act
and thinking about how the way
I act makes other people feel."*

– Fifth Grade Student

Chapter 8
CONSIDERATE

•   •   •

"Being considerate means that you are aware of your surroundings and also aware of how your actions affect others."
– 10th Grade Student

Introduction

Explaining "Considerate" to Students

Social-emotional leaders take the time to think about how their words or actions will affect others. How often do you think about whether your words might hurt others before you speak? How often do you think about whether your actions are making things more difficult for other people? **Considerate means thinking about how your actions make other people feel.** If you are acting out and distracting the class while other students are trying to learn, you are not being considerate of other people. Being considerate involves not only listening to others, but also noticing social cues that communicate how others are thinking and feeling, even if they do not say so outright. Monitoring your words and actions will help you be seen as a person of integrity, as your actions match your spoken values and the way you wish to be seen by others. Additionally, being aware of how your actions impact other people will help you connect and collaborate with them more effectively.

What "Considerate" Looks Like

Leaders who are considerate:

- do not speak or act in ways that hurt or inconvenience others

- reflect on how their actions influence others

- are active listeners

- understand their impact on situations and people

- build rapport with others

- practice emotional intelligence

- are seen as perceptive, adaptive, patient, responsive, and sociable

- try to understand another person's experiences and not make judgments about that person

- can connect with individuals from diverse backgrounds

- can relate to people one-on-one

- ask questions to learn about and understand others

- build confidence in others

- are respectful of others

What Gets in the Way?

If you struggle with being considerate, you might not pick up on cues to how others are thinking and feeling until small misunderstandings grow into problems and conflicts. In the short term, lack of consideration can lead to an absence of trust. Review the following list and note the items that may keep you from being considerate.

- You are unable to pick up on social cues.

- You avoid social situations.

- You are impatient with people.

- Your role models don't model considerate behavior.

- You do not listen to other people.

- You do not think before you speak or act.

- You are self-centered and insensitive to others' needs.

- You are quick to judge other people.

- You tend to focus on the task more than on people.

- You have trouble understanding others' needs or emotions.

Considerate leaders reflect on how their words or actions might make others feel before they speak or act. This helps build connections and relationships with others, making it easier to work together.

Suggestions for Improving "Considerate"

Work with your students to discuss and establish some ways to build competency in this attribute. Below is a list to help support this exercise. Feel free to develop your own strategies or modify these suggestions.

You may also consider doing an activity with your students (see Activity Center for suggestions) or asking them to write about the attribute (see Journal Prompts for suggestions) to help build student understanding.

In conjunction with your students, figure out how you are going to support each other as a group or class to build competency in this leadership attribute.

- **Think before you speak.** Exercise impulse control. Try different strategies, like counting backward from 10, before acting or asking yourself, "If I do this, how will this make other people feel?"

- **Read and adjust.** Social interactions are a back-and-forth affair, not a one-way street. Instead of just waiting to make your point, pay attention to how others react to you and form your response accordingly. If you're not sure how your actions impact someone, ask!

- **Become a people reader.** Learn to read body language and to respond appropriately. Practice all the time: at school, during social events, at home with your family, etc.

- **Keep a red-flag/green-flag journal.** Use a notebook or journal to track "red-flag" and "green-flag" moments. Red flags are the moments when you act without considering the impact your actions could have on others. Green flags are the moments when you consider the impact on others before acting. Keep track of each situation, how you acted, and the impact on others in each situation. Example: If a student hears a rumor about another student, sharing that rumor without thinking about how that student would feel is a red-flag moment, while considering how the student would feel and then choosing not to spread the rumor would be a green-flag moment.

- **Conduct random acts of consideration.** Think about how you can be kind to someone else, and then do it. Act to make someone else's life a little better.

--------------------------------- **Activity Center** ---------------------------------

Here are some suggestions for activities that may be modified to fit your context and the students with whom you are working.

- **Book introduction.** Find a book to read with students that has a character who demonstrates the attribute "considerate" or who would have benefitted from being more considerate, and have students discuss or journal about the character's behavior (see the Suggested Books section of this chapter for books that could be used for this activity).

- **How to be considerate.** Have students work in small groups to develop two short scenes. Both scenes should show the same situation. In the first scene, the characters should not show considerate behavior while in the second they do. Students should make sure the scenes include the impact on others based on the actions taken.

- **Reframing "considerate."** Have students work in pairs. Each partner writes a story in which a person does not show consideration for others. Then, have them exchange stories and rewrite the other person's story, making the protagonists' actions considerate instead of inconsiderate.

- **"Considerate" book group.** Discuss the considerate or inconsiderate actions of characters in any book or short story that students are reading. Discuss why their actions are considerate or inconsiderate and the impact they have on others.

- **Students making a difference.** Working in small groups, students should research children and teens who are making a difference in their community. Students should create a three-minute presentation on their research and how the actions being taken reflect consideration.

- **"Noticing" assignment.** Have students note in a journal considerate and inconsiderate behavior that they witness throughout a regular day. Then, lead a discussion with students about what they noticed. What behaviors did they determine made someone considerate or not? What impact did they perceive on the people involved in the interaction? How did they feel while observing or experiencing this behavior?

- **Not-so-random acts of consideration.** Have students watch a video on random acts of consideration or kindness. (For an example, look up, "Simple act of kindness: student pays off school lunch debt"). Ask students to look for opportunities throughout the week (or month) to be considerate. Have students discuss how it went, what they felt, and what they noticed.

Journal Prompts

Choose one or more of the journal prompts appropriate for the age level you work with. Feel free to modify or extend the prompt. Give students time to reflect on the questions in a personal journal. To extend the exercise, ask students to share their reflections with a peer or small group.

- Think of a time someone went out of their way to help you or listen to you. How did that make you feel? How might you be able to pay this forward?

- Think of a situation in which you were not as considerate as you could have been. How did that affect other people? How could you have acted in a more considerate way?

- Think of people you know who are regularly considerate of others. What are their strategies?

- Reflect on stories that you have read. Describe a situation in which a character acting in a considerate way benefits themselves and/or others. How might you relate the situation to something in your life?

- What is the cost of not being considerate? What are the benefits of being considerate?

- Think of a time when someone did not act in a considerate way toward you. How did this make you feel? How do you wish the person would have acted?

Integrating the Attribute into Your Curriculum

Choose an activity from your planning guide or syllabus. After your students complete the activity, relate the activity back to the "considerate" attribute with a debriefing conversation. Below are suggested questions. Choose or modify questions based on your students' developmental level, your activity, and your context.

This debrief can take the form of a full-group discussion. You might consider giving students time to reflect on their answers with partners or in small groups before asking them to share responses with the larger group. Alternatively, you may decide to ask students to work in small groups to share their responses on flip charts, and then have a gallery walk where students walk around the room and read what other students have written, potentially adding their own comments or thoughts.

- How did the activity help you understand the attribute "considerate"?

- How did you work on being considerate during this activity?

- How did other students demonstrate being considerate during the activity?

- What does it mean to be considerate?

- Why is it important to be considerate?

- How can being considerate make you a better leader?

- How can a lack of being considerate impact leadership?

- How can you develop your ability to be considerate?

- What are some ways you could practice being considerate moving forward?

- How will you demonstrate being considerate in your interactions with others?

- What impact can increasing your ability to be considerate have on you?

- Identify a person, past or present, who demonstrates being considerate. What specific actions demonstrate this person being considerate?

- Identify a book character who demonstrates being considerate. What specific actions does this character do that demonstrate being considerate?

Questions to Assess Understanding

Consider giving the following questions to students to determine if you need to spend more time explaining this attribute.

- What does it mean to be considerate? Give an example of someone you know who is considerate. How does this person demonstrate being considerate?

- What are three things you are going to work on in order to become more considerate?

Suggested Books to Introduce "Considerate"

The books listed below can be used to deepen younger students' understanding of the "considerate" attribute.

- *Being Considerate* by J.L. Donahue & S. Previn

- *Have You Filled a Bucket Today? A Guide to Daily Happiness for Kids* by C. McCloud

- *I Care About Others* by D. Parker

- *The Invisible Boy* by T. Ludwig

- *Last Stop on Market Street* by M. de la Pena

- *Stomp Out Selfishness: Short Stories* by K. Pearson & T. Zowada

- *Those Shoes* by M. Boelts

Additional Resources

This section provides additional places to look for help and advice to develop your personal knowledge, as an adult, about this attribute.

Cartwright, T. (2009). *Changing yourself and your reputation*. Greensboro, NC: Center for Creative Leadership.

Center for Creative Leadership. (2013). *Interpersonal savvy: Building and maintaining solid working relationships*. Greensboro, NC: Author.

Forni, P. M. (2003). *Choosing civility: The twenty-five rules of considerate conduct*. New York, NY: St. Martin's Griffin.

Post, P., & Senning, C. P. (2005). *Emily Post's the gift of good manners: A parent's guide to raising respectful, kind, considerate children*. New York, NY: HarperCollins. Bottom of Form

Scharlatt, H. (2016). *Resolving conflict: Ten steps for turning negatives to positives*. Greensboro, NC: Center for Creative Leadership.

"Being respectful means being able to recognize that some people may not have the same problems as I do, and I try to be understanding by putting myself in their situation."

– 11th Grade Student

Chapter 9
RESPECTFUL

"Respectful means actively thinking about [how] other people might want to be treated differently than you do and treating them the way they want to be treated."
– Eighth Grade Student

"Being respectful means asking someone how they want to be helped."
– Fourth Grade Student

Introduction

Use the information in this section to help you introduce the "respectful" attribute to students. You can use the question stem "How does this attribute make you a better leader?" to start a discussion with your students and to check for comprehension (see Additional Resources for more information to further your personal understanding).

Explaining "Respectful" to Students

Imagine you are working with other students on a group project. Each person in the group is responsible for learning something and then sharing it with the rest of the group. When you are sharing your part, do you want the others to listen quietly and ask questions at the end, or do you want them to ask questions as they arise? Do the other students in the group have the same preference as you? How do you know? How often do you ask others how they want you to respond when they are sharing something with you? Now think about a challenge you may have or something you are struggling with. If you were to share this difficulty with good friends, would you want them to try to problem solve, or do you just want them to say that they understand and feel your pain? How would that friend want you to respond in a similar situation? How could you figure out how they want you to respond? Do you make an effort to understand how people would like to be treated? **Respectful means treating other people the way they wish to be treated (in respect to their preferences, feelings, and emotions).** Being respectful does not mean giving someone your lunch money because they want it or asking someone to do your work for you. Respectfulness is about having the awareness that helps you relate to others in a way that benefits everyone and allows you to work together more effectively. When others see you as compassionate, caring, and empathetic, they are more likely to trust you respect you.

What "Respectful" Looks Like

Leaders who are respectful:

- understand that everyone has unique needs and wants

- are calm and patient when other people are struggling

- are aware that not everyone learns the same way as they do

- help others in the way they want to be helped

- are patient, attentive listeners

- keep confidences

- remain composed in difficult situations

- listen without judgment

- have empathy toward others (feel with someone rather than for someone)

- assume positive intent

- appreciate differences

- expand thinking by working to understand different points of view

What Gets in the Way?

When you are not respectful, you may struggle to connect with others. A lack of respect can inhibit your ability to collaborate. Review the following items and note the items that may keep you from being respectful:

- You spend your time focused on yourself instead of thinking about others.

- You are unaware of the impact of your behavior on others.

- You are unaware of others' needs.

- You think everybody wants to be treated the way you do.

- You act before considering others' needs.

- You are not sensitive to others' emotions.

By treating others the way they would like to be treated, you will be better at building and maintaining relationships, which will help you work better with others.

Suggestions for Improving "Respectful"

Work with your students to discuss and establish some ways to build competency in this attribute. Below is a list to help support this exercise. Feel free to develop your own strategies or modify these suggestions.

You may also consider doing an activity with your students (see Activity Center for suggestions) or asking them to write about the attribute (see Journal Prompts for suggestions) to help build student understanding.

In conjunction with your students, figure out how you are going to support each other as a group or class to build competency in this leadership attribute.

- **Seek first to understand.** Acting or giving out advice without first understanding how the person wishes to be treated can lead to miscommunication and conflict. Try asking other people what type of support they need from you. Actively listen to responses.

- **Learn about differences.** When you are working with people from a different background (ethnicity, religion, geographic location) from yours, make an effort to understand how their backgrounds helped make them who they are.

- **Develop your power of observation.** Become a keen observer of social situations. Watch how people react in different scenarios.

- **Reflect before acting.** Ask yourself if what you are about to do or say reflects how the other person wishes to be treated. For example, if a teacher asks that you raise your hand before speaking and you speak out without raising your hand, then you are not respecting the teacher.

Activity Center

Here are some suggestions for activities that may be modified to fit your context and the students with whom you are working.

- **Book introduction.** Find a book to read with students that has a character who demonstrates the attribute "respectful" or who would have benefitted from being more respectful, and have students discuss or journal about the character's behavior (see the Suggested Books section of this chapter for books that could be used for this activity).

- **Me and you.** Have students work with a partner to describe how they want others to treat them in different circumstances. Sample questions: If you're having a bad day, how do you want other people to respond to you? How do you prefer to work with others in group situations? If you need help, what is the best way to help you? (To give students additional time to think, have them complete the first journal prompt prior to this activity.)

- **Empathy.** Show students the video "Brené Brown on Empathy" (available on YouTube). Ask students how they can practice empathy in their lives. How does having empathy help people be more respectful?

- **Respectful struggles.** Have students identify reasons that can keep people from being respectful. With a peer, have them discuss a situation in which they could have been more respectful and what they could have done differently.

- **Respectful stories.** Have students think about a situation (fictional or real) where a person is respectful. Have students write two stories (or comic strips, videos, plays, etc.), one in which the character is respectful and one in which they are not. In each story, students should focus on the impact of these actions.

- **Peer mediation.** Try to solve a problem that two of your classmates are having by being respectful of both points of view.

Journal Prompts

Choose one or more of the journal prompts appropriate for the age level you work with. Feel free to modify or extend the prompt. Give students time to reflect on the questions in a personal journal. To extend the exercise, ask students to share their reflections with a peer or small group.

- What do others need to know about you in order to treat you respectfully? Think about the following questions: If you're having a bad day, how do you want other people to respond to you? How do you prefer to work with others in group situations? If you need help, what is the best way to help you?

- Think of a time when you have received respectful treatment from someone. How did that make you feel toward that person?

- Think of a situation in which you were not treated the way you wanted to be. How did it make you feel? How did you respond? How did you want to be treated?

- Think of a conflict situation you've experienced. How could you have handled that situation by being respectful?

- How could you be more respectful to your parents? Your teachers? Your peers?

Integrating the Attribute into Your Curriculum

Choose an activity from your planning guide or syllabus. After your students complete the activity, relate the activity back to the "respectful" attribute with a debriefing conversation. Below are suggested questions. Choose or modify questions based on your students' developmental level, your activity, and your context.

This debrief can take the form of a full-group discussion. You might consider giving students time to reflect on their answers with partners or in small groups before asking them to share responses with the larger group. Alternatively, you may decide to ask students to work in small groups to share their responses on flip charts, and then have a gallery walk where students walk around the room and read what other students have written, potentially adding their own comments or thoughts.

- How did the activity help you understand the attribute "respectful"?

- How did you work on being respectful during this activity?

- How did other students demonstrate being respectful during the activity?

- What does it mean to be respectful?

- Why is it important to be respectful?

- How can being respectful make you a better leader?

- How can a lack of being respectful impact leadership?

- How can you become more respectful?

- What are some ways you could practice being respectful moving forward?

- How will you demonstrate being respectful in your interactions with others?

- What impact can increasing your ability to be respectful have on you?

- Identify a person, past or present, who demonstrates being respectful. What specific actions does this person do that demonstrate being respectful?

- Identify a book character who demonstrates being respectful. What specific actions does this character do that demonstrate being respectful?

Questions to Assess Understanding

Consider giving the following questions to students to determine if you need to spend more time explaining this attribute.

- What does it mean to be respectful? Give an example of someone you know who is respectful. How does this person demonstrate being respectful?

- What are three things you are going to work on in order to become more respectful?

Suggested Books to Introduce "Respectful"

The books listed below can be used to deepen younger students' understanding of the "respectful" attribute.

- *Be Kind* by P. Z. Miller & J. Hill

- *Chrysanthemum* by K. Henkes

- *Do Unto Otters: A Book About Manners* by L. Keller

- *The Golden Rule* by I. Cooper & G. Swiatkowska

- *How Can I Help? A Book about Caring* by R. Nelson

- *I Just Don't Like the Sound of No!* by J. Cook & K. De Weerd

- *I Show Respect!* by D. Parker

- *I Walk with Vanessa: A Story about a Simple Act of Kindness* by Kerascoët

- *My Mouth Is a Volcano!* by J. Cook

- *The Rabbit Listened* by C. Doerrfeld

- *Respect and Take Care of Things* by C.J. Meiners

- *Stand in My Shoes: Kids Learning about Empathy* by R. Sornson & S. Johannes

- *We're All Wonders* by R.J. Palacio

- *Why Should I? A Book about Respect* by S. Graves, E. Carletti, & D. Guicciardini

Additional Resources

This section provides additional places to look for help and advice to develop your personal knowledge, as an adult, about this attribute.

Borba, M. (2016). *UnSelfie: Why empathetic kids succeed in our all-about-me world.* New York, NY: Touchstone.

Center for Creative Leadership. (n.d.). *Relationship skills can be learned.* [Podcast]. Greensboro, NC: Author.

Grant, A. (2013). *Give and take: Why helping others drives our success.* New York, NY: Viking.

Iacoboni, M. (2008). *Mirroring people: The science of empathy and how we connect with people.* New York, NY: Farrar, Straus, and Giroux.

Klann, G. (2007). *Building character: Strengthening the heart of good leadership.* San Francisco, CA: Jossey-Bass.

Klann, G. (n.d.). *Leadership character: Five influential attributes.* [Podcast]. Center for Creative Leadership. Greensboro, NC. Retrieved from https://www.ccl.org/multimedia/podcast/leadership-character-five-influential-attributes/

Meshanko, P. (2013). *The respect effect: Using the science of neuroleadership to inspire a more loyal and productive workplace.* New York, NY: McGraw-Hill.

"[Being accepting means] respecting and acknowledging the humanity of everyone."

– 10th Grade Student

Chapter 10
ACCEPTING

• • •

"A lot of people judge people by how they look; for example, their skin tone or how pretty they look. People judge other people because they think if they are pretty they are nice. [Being accepting means] never judge the book by its cover or the way people look."
– Third Grade Student

Introduction

Explaining "Accepting" to Students

At school, and in life, you are surrounded by people with different beliefs, interests, genders, cultures, abilities, and backgrounds than yours. How often do you work with people who have different ideas and skills than you? How much time do you spend trying to understand another person's culture or point of view? Do others see you as someone who is understanding and non-judgmental? **Accepting means appreciating the views of others, even if they are different from your own.** When you are accepting, you are able to work better with a wide variety of other people. To be accepting, it is important to recognize and respect that not all people think the same way you do. If you are accepting, then you are willing to listen to others' opinions, even if they differ from yours. This will help you work better with others, build stronger relationships, and expand your understanding of the world around you. Leaders need to be able to work with many people from different backgrounds.

What "Accepting" Looks Like

Leaders who are accepting:

- appreciate others' viewpoints even when they are different from their own

- move beyond stereotypes and treat each person as uniquely gifted

- remain aware of their own biases and cultural influences

- understand how individual differences strengthen the community

- strive to see problems and seek solutions from many different perspectives

- are seen as interested in other people, respectful, perceptive, curious, open-minded, adaptive, and good listeners

- seek opportunities to learn about different cultures and customs

- try to understand what other people think without judging them

- understand differences among people with varied backgrounds

- ask questions to learn about and understand others

What Gets in the Way?

Without acceptance, you will lose out on opportunities to learn from people who have different experiences than your own. Review the following list and note the items that might be keeping you from being accepting.

- You have had limited exposure to different cultures.

- You have not had diverse experiences.

- You surround yourself with people who are like you.

- You are rigid and set in your ways.

- You tend to see problems or issues from a narrow perspective.

- You make incorrect assumptions about what people need.

- You are inconsistent or unfair in your treatment of people.

- You do not take the time to understand others who are different from you.

If you are accepting of others' views, you open yourself up to learning more and broadening your perspective. This will allow you to work more effectively with others to find unique solutions to challenges.

Suggestions for Improving "Accepting"

Work with your students to discuss and establish some ways to build competency in this attribute. Below is a list to help support this exercise. Feel free to develop your own strategies or modify these suggestions.

You may also consider doing an activity with your students (see Activity Center for suggestions) or asking them to write about the attribute (see Journal Prompts for suggestions) to help build student understanding.

In conjunction with your students, figure out how you are going to support each other as a group or class to build competency in this leadership attribute.

- **Experience different cultures where you are.** You don't have to travel the world to experience culture firsthand—odds are you can experience new things and unique people in your school and community.

- **Read about other cultures.** Research people who have different backgrounds than you.

- **Challenge yourself culturally.** Are you particularly inexperienced with a specific group of people? Try to get to know someone who is from a different culture than you. Introduce yourself and ask respectful questions.

- **Learn cultural competence from others.** Seek out peers and adults who demonstrate a high level of cultural awareness and experience, and notice how this awareness is reflected in their interactions.

- **Examine your cultural foundations.** Study and reflect on your own cultural background. Consider how your cultural identity influences your perspective and behaviors.

- **Foster inclusion from the start.** Ask your peers to brainstorm ways to help new students or group or team members feel included. Some ideas to get you started:

» Look for something that new team members have in common with you, like extracurricular interests.

» Ask new people to talk about their previous experiences.

- **Learn another language.** It's natural to rely on your native language for most communication. But if you learn another language, you create an opportunity to make a personal connection with people from other cultures. Even a basic understanding of another language can provide a deeper appreciation of the beliefs of other cultures.

- **Anticipate cultural differences.** Be alert to the role of cultural background in your school and in your interactions with your peers.

Activity Center

Here are some suggestions for activities that may be modified to fit your context and the students with whom you are working.

- **Book introduction.** Find a book to read with students that has a character who demonstrates the attribute "accepting" or who would have benefitted from being more accepting, and have students discuss or journal about the character's behavior (see the Suggested Books section of this chapter for books that could be used for this activity).

- **Practice people watching.** Tell students the following: "Watching others is a good way to learn more about how people behave, and those observations can give you a chance to think about how you respond to behavior tied to differences. You can learn about such things as how different cultures view personal space, how different people use public space, etc. Record your observations like a scientist, writing down exactly what is happening without judgement." Then ask students to share their observations with a partner and discuss what they noticed about how being passive observers helped them to be more accepting.

- **Why not accept?** Have students identify reasons that can keep people from being accepting. Have them discuss with a peer a situation in which they could have been more accepting and what they could have done differently.

- **Acceptance stories.** Have students think about a situation (fictional or real) where a person displays acceptance. Have students write two stories (or comic strips, videos, plays, etc.), one in which the character is accepting and one in which they are not. In each story, students should focus on the impact of these actions.

Journal Prompts

Choose one or more of the journal prompts appropriate for the age level you work with. Feel free to modify or extend the prompt. Give students time to reflect on the questions in a personal journal. To extend the exercise, ask students to share their reflections with a peer or small group.

- When have others made you feel valued and appreciated for who you are? What did they do to make you feel that way?

- Think of a situation in which you were not accepted. How did it make you feel? How did you respond?

- Think of someone whose perspective or background is different from yours. What can you learn from that difference?

- What types of diversity do you value? How can appreciating diversity help you be a better social-emotional leader?

- Are there any stereotypes that you're trying to overcome? How do you react when someone makes assumptions based on how you look or where you're from?

- How can you show others that you appreciate them sharing points of view that are different from your own?

Integrating the Attribute into Your Curriculum

Choose an activity from your planning guide or syllabus. After your students complete the activity, relate the activity back to the "accepting" attribute with a debriefing conversation. Below are suggested questions. Choose or modify questions based on your students' developmental level, your activity, and your context.

This debrief can take the form of a full-group discussion. You might consider giving students time to reflect on their answers with partners or in small groups before asking them to share responses with the larger group. Alternatively, you may decide to ask students to work in small groups to share their responses on flip charts, and then have a gallery walk where students walk around the room and read what other students have written, potentially adding their own comments or thoughts.

- How did the activity help you understand the attribute "accepting"?

- How did you work on being accepting during this activity?

- How did other students demonstrate being accepting during the activity?

- What does it mean to be accepting?

- Why is it important to be accepting?

- How can being accepting make you a better leader?

- How can a lack of being accepting impact leadership?

- How can you become more accepting?

- What are some ways you could practice being accepting moving forward?

- How will you demonstrate being accepting in your interactions with others?

- What impact can increasing your ability to be accepting have on you?

- Identify a person, past or present, who demonstrates being accepting. What specific actions does this person do that demonstrate being accepting?

- Identify a book character who demonstrates being accepting. What specific actions does this character do that demonstrate being accepting?

Questions to Assess Understanding

Consider giving the following questions to students to determine if you need to spend more time explaining this attribute.

- What does it mean to be accepting? Give an example of someone you know who is accepting. How does this person demonstrate being accepting?

- What are three things you are going to work on in order to become more accepting?

Suggested Books to Introduce "Accepting"

The books listed below can be used to deepen younger students' understanding of the "accepting" attribute.

- *All Are Welcome* by A. Penfold & S. Kaufman

- *Bein' with You This Way* by W. Nicola-Lisa & M. Bryant

- *Chocolate Milk, Por Favor! Celebrating Diversity with Empathy* by M. Dismondy & D. Farrell

- *Chrysanthemum* by K. Henkes

- *I Accept You as You Are!* by D. Parker

- *The One, the Only Magnificent Me!* by D. Haseltine

- *Out of My Mind* by S.M. Draper

- *Same, Same but Different* by J.S. Kostecki-Shaw

- *The Sneetches and Other Stories* by Dr. Seuss

- *The True Story of the Three Little Pigs* by J. Scieszka

- *We Are All Alike... We Are All Different* by the Cheltenham Elementary School Kindergartners

- *Who We Are! All About Being the Same and Being Different* by R. H. Harris & N. B. Westcott

- *Wishtree* by K. Applegate & C. Santoso

- *You Are (Not) Small* by A. Kang

Additional Resources

This section provides additional places to look for help and advice to develop your personal knowledge, as an adult, about this attribute.

Bullard, S. (1996). *Teaching tolerance: Raising open-minded, empathetic children.* New York, NY: Doubleday.

Deal, J., & Prince, D. W. (2003). *Developing cultural adaptability: How to work across differences.* Greensboro, NC: Center for Creative Leadership.

Ernst, C., & Chrobot-Mason, D. (2010). *Boundary spanning leadership: Six practices for solving problems, driving innovation, and transforming organizations.* New York, NY: McGraw-Hill.

Gay, G. (2018). *Culturally responsive teaching: Theory, research, and practice (3rd ed.).* New York, NY: Teachers College Press.

Grant, A. M. (2016). *Originals: How non-conformists move the world.* New York, NY: Viking.

Hannum, Kelly M. (2007). *Social identity: Knowing yourself, leading others.* Greensboro, NC: Center for Creative Leadership.

Hannum, K. M., McFeeters, B. B., & Booysen, L. (2010). *Leading across differences: Cases and perspectives.* San Francisco, CA: Pfeiffer.

Tatum, B. D. (2007). *Can we talk about race? And other conversations in an era of school resegregation.* Boston, MA: Beacon Press.

CHANGING YOUR WORLD

The choices that you make influence the world around you. You can purposefully make a positive difference by motivating, uniting, and engaging others towards accomplishing a goal. This section includes information about the following leadership attributes:

ATTRIBUTES	DEFINITIONS
Visionary	creates a compelling vision and inspires others to follow it
Motivating	unites a group of people to work together toward a common goal
Encouraging	encourages others to take on leadership roles
Confident	steps up and takes charge when it is needed

"[Visionary means] to look ahead and think in the future. It is Martin Luther King Jr. saying, 'I have a dream that all people are equal.'"

– Fourth Grade Student

Chapter 11
VISIONARY

• • •

"Visionary means to have visions that do good for a large or small community. With this vision, you will spend time working to make it true."
– Sixth Grade Student

"Visionary is applying new ideas (created by yourself or others) to make a change in the world around you. This is about learning to recognize and make use of strong imagination."
– 11th Grade Student

Introduction

Explaining "Visionary" to Students

An important aspect of leadership is being able to create energy and enthusiasm around ideas. How often do you feel passionate about your ideas? How often do you share them with others? Are others inspired when you share ideas? **Visionary means being able to create a compelling plan for the future and inspire others to follow it.** When conveyed with passion and purpose, your vision can inspire others to take action. Visionary leaders imagine the future and can see new possibilities. They have a relentless belief that enacting their vision will lead to a positive difference in their world. This draws people together to work toward making that vision a reality. Being visionary makes you a better social-emotional leader, because you are able to inspire others.

What "Visionary" Looks Like

Visionary leaders:

- can promote an idea or vision and persuade others to see a different perspective

- understand what motivates people in order to share a vision in a way that's meaningful to others

- can influence others without using formal authority

- are seen as persuasive and inspirational, sparking others to join their efforts

- imagine the future and can see new possibilities

- draw people together to engage in the vision

- tell stories to communicate the vision meaningfully and memorably

- model behavior that turns vision into action

- are insightful, intuitive, curious, inventive, focused, passionate, inspired, persuasive, inspirational, energetic, enthusiastic, and engaging

What Gets in the Way?

Without vision, it is hard to inspire people or get them to work together toward a common goal. Review the following list and note the items that may keep you from being visionary.

- You are not assertive.

- You rely on other people to create a vision of the future.

- Your communication doesn't portray your vision in a compelling way.

- You grow impatient and frustrated with resistance to your ideas.

- You do not interact enough with the people you want to inspire.

- You talk about your vision without taking action.

- You get frustrated and give up.

- You are not enthusiastic about your ideas.

A social-emotional leader imagines the future, communicates their vision, and works with others to make it happen.

Suggestions for Improving "Visionary" ————————————

Work with your students to discuss and establish some ways to build competency in this attribute. Below is a list to help support this exercise. Feel free to develop your own strategies or modify these suggestions.

You may also consider doing an activity with your students (see Activity Center for suggestions) or asking them to write about the attribute (see Journal Prompts for suggestions) to help build student understanding.

In conjunction with your students, figure out how you are going to support each other as a group or class to build competency in this leadership attribute.

- **Write your future.** Imagine yourself a few years from now. Describe how you have achieved all of the things you set out to do. What are people saying about you? What will they say next?

- **Map your vision.** How will your story unfold? What steps will you take along the way? How will you help others? Who will help you? What obstacles will you overcome?

- **Use imagery.** Use pictures, tell stories, and make use of impressions and metaphors to powerfully describe the situations that lie before you and your peers, and encourage others to build on your vision with their own supporting ideas.

- **Engage your classmates in exploring a vision.** Get together with peers and others to talk about possible service activities. Bounce ideas off each other until the right vision emerges—one that sparks deep passion and commitment.

- **Tell a story.** When you tell a story to illustrate your vision, people will find it easier to recall.

- **Perfect your "elevator speech."** What compelling vision can you describe in 25 seconds, or during the time a typical elevator ride takes? Practice communicating your vision in a clear, brief way. Be prepared to talk about it everywhere.

- **Learn how to use multiple forms of media.** The more channels of communication you use, the better the chance people have of hearing and understanding your vision.

Activity Center

Here are some suggestions for activities that may be modified to fit your context and the students with whom you are working.

- **Book introduction.** Find a book to read with students that has a character who demonstrates the attribute "visionary" or who would have benefitted from being more visionary, and have students discuss or journal about the character's behavior (see the Suggested Books section of this chapter for books that could be used for this activity).

- **Vision board.** Step 1: Have students create a collage with words and images that describe their vision for their future. Step 2: Have students write a brief explanation to accompany their collage, describing their vision for the future. This explanation should reflect the passion they have for their vision. Step 3: Ask students to share their vision with a partner. Step 4: Have a gallery walk, where all collages and explanations are on display, and everyone gets a chance to look at all of them.

- **Vision for the classroom.** Work with students to create a vision for improving their learning environment. Have students create a compelling presentation for the principal, explaining their vision and how it will make a positive difference.

- **Inspirational speech.** Have students write an inspirational speech (could be a poem, spoken word, etc.) titled "This Is My Vision for the Future" to share with the class.

- **Influence me.** Have students get into groups of three and take turns attempting to influence each other about a particular topic. Provide the following example: "You want to go to a movie that your friend is not interested in seeing. What would motivate your friend to go with you? How could you influence your friend to go along?" Debrief with students how this experience felt for them.

- **TED Talks.** Find a developmentally appropriate TED Talk that promotes a clear vision of the future. Show this video to your class. Have students identify all the components that make the speech visionary (including content, body language, passion, word choice, etc.).

- **Students who are changing the world.** Have students do some research to identify youth who are changing the world through their vision and actions. Ask students to create a presentation introducing these visionaries and sharing their impact.

- **Contemporary visionaries.** Ask students to choose a great visionary of our time. Ask students to find a video of this individual making a speech or giving an interview. What makes this person visionary?

- **Visionaries in history.** Have students choose a visionary historical figure related to a time period they are studying in class and create a presentation explaining how this person was a visionary.

Journal Prompts

Choose one or more of the journal prompts appropriate for the age level you work with. Feel free to modify or extend the prompt. Give students time to reflect on the questions in a personal journal. To extend the exercise, ask students to share their reflections with a peer or small group.

- Describe your vision of a change you would like to see in your school or community. What excites you most about your vision? How could you help make that change happen? What about it do you believe will inspire others?

- What is the craziest idea you've ever had? How did you share it with others? How did other people respond to it?

- Who was the most inspiring person you have ever met? What was their vision, and how did they communicate it?

- Create a storyboard (draw a comic strip) illustrating a change you would like to see in your school or community.

- Can you think of an idea you had that became a reality? What did it take to help bring this idea to life?

- How old will you be in twenty years? Make a list, write a narrative, or create an illustration that represents your vision of yourself twenty years from now. Where will you live? What will you do for a job? What types of people will be your friends? What will your typical day look like? Think about the goals you will need to set (and accomplish) for one year from now, three years from now, five years from now, and ten years from now in order to achieve this vision.

Integrating the Attribute into Your Curriculum

Choose an activity from your planning guide or syllabus. After your students complete the activity, relate the activity back to the "visionary" attribute with a debriefing conversation. Below are suggested questions. Choose or modify questions based on your students' developmental level, your activity, and your context.

This debrief can take the form of a full-group discussion. You might consider giving students time to reflect on their answers with partners or in small groups before asking them to share responses with the larger group. Alternatively, you may decide to ask students to work in small groups to share their responses on flip charts, and then have a gallery walk where students walk around the room and read what other students have written, potentially adding their own comments or thoughts.

- How did the activity help you understand the attribute "visionary"?

- How did you work on being visionary during this activity?

- How did other students demonstrate being visionary during the activity?

- What does it mean to be visionary?

- Why is it important to be visionary?

- How can being visionary make you a better social-emotional leader?

- How can a lack of being visionary impact leadership?

- How can you work on developing your skills in this leadership attribute?

- What are some ways you could practice being visionary moving forward?

- How will you demonstrate being visionary in your interactions with others?

- What impact can increasing your ability to be visionary have on you?

- Identify a person, past or present, who demonstrates being visionary. What specific actions demonstrate this person being visionary?

- Identify a book character who demonstrates being visionary. What specific actions does this character take that demonstrate being visionary?

Questions to Assess Understanding

Consider giving the following questions to students to determine if you need to spend more time explaining this attribute.

- What does it mean to be visionary? Give an example of someone you know who is a visionary leader. How does this person demonstrate being visionary?

- What are three things you are going to work on in order to become a more visionary leader?

Suggested Books to Introduce "Visionary"

The books listed below can be used to deepen younger students' understanding of the "visionary" attribute.

- *Anything Is Possible* by G. Belloni, W. Anselmi, & M. Trevisan

- *How to Catch a Star* by O. Jeffers

- *If I Were in Charge…* by T. Stead

- *Little Dreamers: Visionary Women around the World* by V. Harrison

- *Little Leaders: Bold Women in Black History* by V. Harrison

- *Sam and Dave Dig a Hole* by M. Barnett

Additional Resources

This section provides additional places to look for help and advice to develop your personal knowledge, as an adult, about this attribute.

Cartwright, T., & Baldwin, D. (2006). *Communicating your vision.* Greensboro, NC: Center for Creative Leadership.

Cialdini, R. B. (2007). *Influence: The psychology of persuasion.* New York, NY: Collins.

Criswell, C., & Cartwright, T. (2010). *Creating a vision.* Greensboro, NC: Center for Creative Leadership.

Goldsmith, M., & Reiter, M. (2014). *What got you here won't get you there.* New York, NY: MJF Books.

Maxwell, J. C. (2005). *The 360 degree leader: Developing your influence from anywhere in the organization.* Nashville, TN: Nelson Business.

Schachter, L., & Cheatham, R. (2016). *Selling vision: The x-xy-y formula for driving results by selling change.* New York, NY: McGraw-Hill Education.

Scharlatt, H. (2008). *Selling your ideas to your organization.* Greensboro, NC: Center for Creative Leadership.

Scharlatt, H., & Smith, R. (2011). *Influence: Gaining commitment, getting results (2nd ed.).* Greensboro, NC: Center for Creative Leadership.

Sinek, S. (2009). *Start with why: How great leaders inspire everyone to take action.* New York, NY: Portfolio.

"[Motivating] means trying to understand how others think and feel, and even if one does not completely understand others, they listen and communicate to reach a collaborative level."

– 10th Grade Student

Chapter 12
MOTIVATING

• • •

"[Motivating] means knowing how to get people to work together to achieve your goal."
– Eighth Grade Student

Introduction

Explaining "Motivating" to Students

No one works alone, especially not leaders. The role of a social-emotional leader is to be able to produce results through working with others. This is not an easy task—managing teamwork is complicated. How often are you able to pull people together around a common goal? Are you able to work with others to establish a clear outcome and process? Are you able to create a space in which all people feel comfortable communicating honestly and transparently in order to move the work forward? **Motivating means having the ability to get a group of people to work together toward a common goal.** Motivating leaders can ultimately transform a group of individuals into a team committed to meeting specific goals.

What "Motivating" Looks Like

Motivating leaders:

- promote camaraderie (positive relationships) among group members

- work with the group to define goals and establish clear steps to accomplish them

- engage everyone in the group

- set the expectation that everyone will come together to tackle a challenge

- facilitate group efforts and learning

- hold group members accountable

- are seen as positive, affirming, inspiring, challenging, and fair

- size up strengths of individual group members and look for ways to leverage those strengths

- give people a sense of their individual purpose

- provide and seek feedback and guidance

What Gets in the Way?

When leaders are not able to motivate others, their group may not be successful in achieving its goals. Review the following list and note the items that may keep you from being motivating.

- You do not work with others in your group to create a shared understanding of your group goal.

- You focus more on tasks than people.

- You are afraid to speak up when you disagree with others.

- You do not trust the people who work with you.

- Your group members do not trust each other.

- You ignore deep conflicts affecting the group.

- You feel like you have to do everything yourself.

- You do not permit others in the group to ask questions.

- You spend too much time getting consensus and fail to exercise strong decision-making skill when it is needed.

- Your group members are uncertain about results and feel pulled in different directions by competing goals.

- Your group members work in isolation and are uncertain about how their tasks fit into the larger picture and goal.

- Your group members put their own interests ahead of the group and contribute only when it is easy.

Your work as a social-emotional leader involves bringing people together, creating a shared understanding of the group goal, creating a clear plan for how you will work together to accomplish your goal, and providing an environment where people value other members of the group and are committed to the group goals.

Suggestions for Improving "Motivating"

Work with your students to discuss and establish some ways to build competency in this attribute. Below is a list to help support this exercise. Feel free to develop your own strategies or modify these suggestions.

You may also consider doing an activity with your students (see Activity Center for suggestions) or asking them to write about the attribute (see Journal Prompts for suggestions) to help build student understanding.

In conjunction with your students, figure out how you are going to support each other as a group or class to build competency in this leadership attribute.

- **Set and communicate the group's direction—together.** Work with your group to develop a shared understanding of the group's goals. Align the group's work with its goals. Discuss what each group member needs to be able to accomplish their goals.

- **Regularly check progress.** Gather feedback or data to make sure the group is on track toward meeting its goals.

- **Get to know your group members.** Connect with group members to learn more about their special skills, perspectives, and approaches to their work. Find out what they know and how you can help them have a greater impact on the group's goals.

- **Create consensus.** Work together to define the responsibilities of each member of the group and decide on group norms (how you will show up when you work together). This will ensure consistency and prevent conflicts before they start.

- **Celebrate.** Find reasons to celebrate. Make your group work fun and rewarding.

Activity Center

Here are some suggestions for activities that may be modified to fit your context and the students with whom you are working.

- **Book introduction.** Find a book to read with students that has a character who demonstrates the attribute "motivating" or who would have benefitted from being more motivating, and have students discuss or journal about the character's behavior (see the Suggested Books section of this chapter for books that could be used for this activity).

- **Motivating – Group Self-Assessment.** Have students work with their group or team to assess their team using the Motivating – Group Self-Assessment (p. 150).

- **Motivating reflection.** Ask students to think of a time someone influenced them to do something that ended up being very good for them even though it was not something they wanted to do at first. Ask them to reflect upon these questions: How did this person change your mind? What did this experience teach you about how you are personally motivated? Ask students to share these ideas with a partner or in groups of three.

- **Motivating interview.** Ask students to think about someone they respect because of their ability to get others to work together toward a goal. Have them set up a time to interview this person and collect information about how they motivate others. Some questions they might use: Have you always wanted to do the kind of work you do now? What keeps you interested in the work that you do? How do you motivate others to achieve goals? Ask students to make a video or write a short biography of this person, focusing on how they motivate others.

Motivating – Group Self-Assessment

Have you been inspired when witnessing a sports team win a championship or a theatre group put on an amazing production? In these situations, individual players become part of a greater whole that amplifies their individual contributions. Great teams and groups cultivate a culture that encourages coaching each other, and they do not miss opportunities to get better. Rate your group on each of the following characteristics of successful groups from 1 (nonexistent) to 7 (always present). Add any additional characteristics that you think are important and are missing from this list.

CHARACTERISTIC OF SUCCESSFUL GROUPS	YOUR GROUP SCORE
Unified vision and purpose	
Willingness to adapt	
Love of learning and development	
Ability to have fun while remaining focused on goals	
Passionate about collaboration and improvement	
Regular communication	
Resilience (ability to bounce back from setbacks)	
Celebrating success and learning from mistakes	
Prioritize team or group outcomes	

Discuss the following with your team or group:

- In which two or three characteristics is our team/group the strongest?

- On which characteristics did our team score the lowest?

- What can we do better that will help us to be a more successful team?

- What can each person do individually to support our improvements?

Based on your discussion, create a "successful team/group" plan for the future that will keep group members motivated.

Journal Prompts

Choose one or more of the journal prompts appropriate for the age level you work with. Feel free to modify or extend the prompt. Give students time to reflect on the questions in a personal journal. To extend the exercise, ask students to share their reflections with a peer or small group.

- Think about a dream project you would like to lead others in achieving (for example, creating a school garden). Describe the project. How would you motivate a group of people to work together on this project?

- Think of a challenging group project that you were part of. Describe the challenges. What could you have done to help the group members work better together?

- Write about the benefits of group work versus individual work. How is self-motivation different from motivating others?

- Think about somebody (in real life or in the media) who is a motivating leader. What characteristics do they display? How do they motivate others?

- What strengths do you have in motivating a group of people to work together? What challenges do you face in motivating others? How could you improve your skills at becoming a more motivating leader?

Integrating the Attribute into Your Curriculum ———

Choose an activity from your planning guide or syllabus. After your students complete the activity, relate the activity back to the "motivating" attribute with a debriefing conversation. Below are suggested questions. Choose or modify questions based on your students' developmental level, your activity, and your context.

This debrief can take the form of a full-group discussion. You might consider giving students time to reflect on their answers with partners or in small groups before asking them to share responses with the larger group. Alternatively, you may decide to ask students to work in small groups to share their responses on flip charts, and then have a gallery walk where students walk around the room and read what other students have written, potentially adding their own comments or thoughts.

- How did the activity help you understand the attribute "motivating"?

- How did you work on being motivating during this activity?

- How did other students demonstrate being motivating during the activity?

- What does it mean to be motivating?

- Why is it important to be motivating?

- How can being motivating make you a better leader?

- How can a lack of being motivating impact leadership?

- How can you work on becoming more motivating?

- What are some ways you could practice being motivating moving forward?

- How will you demonstrate being motivating in your interactions with others?

- What impact can increasing your ability to be motivating have on you?

- Identify a person, past or present, who demonstrates being motivating. What specific actions demonstrate this person being motivating?

- Identify a book character who demonstrates being motivating. What specific actions of this character demonstrate being motivating?

Questions to Assess Understanding

Consider giving the following questions to students to determine if you need to spend more time explaining this attribute.

- What does it mean to be motivating? Give an example of someone you know who is a motivating leader. How does this person demonstrate being motivating?

- What are three things you are going to work on in order to become a more motivating leader?

Suggested Books to Introduce "Motivating"

The books listed below can be used to deepen younger students' understanding of the "motivating" attribute.

- *A Whistle for Willie* by E. J. Keats

- *Book Uncle and Me* by U. Krishnaswami & J. Swaney

- *Brave Irene* by W. Steig

- *Click, Clack, Moo Cows That Type* by D. Cronin & B. Lewin

- *How to Catch a Star* by O. Jeffers

- *I am Martin Luther King Jr.* by B. Meltzer & C. Eliopoulos

- *Swimmy* by L. Lionni

Additional Resources

This section provides additional places to look for help and advice to develop your personal knowledge, as an adult, about this attribute.

Godin, S. (2008). *Tribes: We need you to lead us*. New York, NY: Portfolio.

Kanaga, K., & Browning, H. (2003). *Maintaining team performance*. Greensboro, NC: Center for Creative Leadership.

Kanaga, K., & Kossler, M.E. (2001). *How to form a team: Five keys to high performance.* Greensboro, NC: Center for Creative Leadership.

Kanaga, K., & Prestridge, S. (2002). *How to launch a team: Start right for success.* Greensboro, NC: Center for Creative Leadership.

Klann, G. (2004). *Building your team's morale, pride, and spirit.* Greensboro, NC: Center for Creative Leadership.

Kossler, M. E., & Kanaga, K. (2001). *Do you really need a team?* Greensboro, NC: Center for Creative Leadership.

Lindoerfer, D. (2008). *Raising sensitive issues in a team.* Greensboro, NC: Center for Creative Leadership.

Runde, C.E., & Flanagan, T.A. (2008). *Building conflict competent teams.* San Francisco, CA: Jossey-Bass.

Sinek, S. (2014). *Leaders eat last: Why some teams pull together and others don't.* New York, NY: Penguin.

Sinek, S. (2009). *Start with why: How great leaders inspire everyone to take action.* New York, NY: Portfolio.

Scharlatt, H. & Smith, R. (2011). *Influence: gaining commitment, getting results (2nd ed.).* Greensboro, NC: Center for Creative Leadership.

"I understand what my friends are good at and I encourage them to be leaders."

– Fifth Grade Student

Chapter 13
ENCOURAGING

"[Encouraging] means that when you are working in a group project, you ask people who are good at certain things (like putting together PowerPoint presentations) to lead that part of the work."
– 10th Grade Student

Introduction

Use the information in this section to help you introduce the "encouraging" attribute to students. You can use the question stem "How does this attribute make you a better leader?" to start a discussion with your students and to check for comprehension (see Additional Resources for more information to further your personal understanding).

Explaining "Encouraging" to Students

Social-emotional leaders understand that sharing leadership with others allows the group to accomplish greater things. These leaders realize that all group members have unique strengths to offer, and they need to feel empowered to contribute to the work of the group. How often do you recognize the strengths of others? How often do you invite others to share leadership? **Encouraging means empowering others to take on leadership roles.** Encouraging leaders promote collaboration and instill a sense of trust, emboldening others to contribute to important tasks. Encouraging leaders are able to understand the strengths of others and motivate them to use those strengths to help accomplish the goals of the group. When you are encouraging, you give others the authority to make decisions and take independent action. This will help ensure the groups' success, because people will be more committed to the collective goal.

What "Encouraging" Looks Like

Encouraging leaders:

- make sure all those involved know their own and others' roles

- explain the context of the task (challenges, resources, and prior history)

- involve the group in identifying the desired process for completing the task and determining its outcomes

- encourage others to make decisions and take independent action

- share responsibility with others

- provide guidance when needed

- give others the space to accomplish tasks in their own way (autonomy)

- are seen as supportive, trustworthy, empowering, engaging, and aware

- learn what interests or excites people and encourage that kind of work if possible

- support risk-taking and learning from mistakes

- size up strengths of individual group members and look for ways to leverage those strengths

What Gets in the Way?

When you are not encouraging, you may see the performance of the group decrease as one person tries to lead everything. Additionally, if you are the person who is trying to lead everything, you may find yourself exhausted and overwhelmed. Review the following list and note the items that might be keeping you from being encouraging.

- You have not figured out how the work should be done, and you are unwilling to ask others for their suggestions.

- You have been burned in the past by giving up too much control.

- You put too much responsibility and pressure on yourself.

- You underestimate the capabilities of others, giving them fewer responsibilities than they are able to take on.

- You hold onto work so you can receive the recognition.

- You believe that other people cannot do the work as well as you can.

- You do not want others to outshine you—to know more or to be seen as better than you.

- You order others to do things instead of sharing leadership.

Understanding the unique talents that others bring to the group, and encouraging them to use these talents through sharing leadership roles will help you all accomplish your group goals.

Suggestions for Improving "Encouraging"

Work with your students to discuss and establish some ways to build competency in this attribute. Below is a list to help support this exercise. Feel free to develop your own strategies or modify these suggestions.

You may also consider doing an activity with your students (see Activity Center for suggestions) or asking them to write about the attribute (see Journal Prompts for suggestions) to help build student understanding.

In conjunction with your students, figure out how you are going to support each other as a group or class to build competency in this leadership attribute.

- **Get to know other people's strengths and abilities.** Take time to figure out what other people are good at. Spend time observing others. Ask your peers what type of work they enjoy doing.

- **Compliment strengths.** When you notice that someone else is good at something, show them you have noticed. Make sure to be genuine and authentic.

- **Be vulnerable.** Tell other people when you struggle with leading. Ask for support and encouragement.

- **Encourage others to be leaders.** Ask other people to take on responsibilities.

- **Listen to all voices.** Make sure to involve your entire group in identifying the desired process for completing the task and determining its outcomes.

Activity Center

Here are some suggestions for activities that may be modified to fit your context and the students with whom you are working.

- **Book introduction.** Find a book to read with students that has a character who demonstrates the attribute "encouraging" or who would have benefitted from being more encouraging, and have students discuss or journal about the character's behavior (see the Suggested Books section of this chapter for books that could be used for this activity).

- **Why share leadership?** Have students work in groups to create role plays about scenarios where leadership is shared and where it is not. What is the difference in outcomes when leadership is shared?

- **Human Knot.** Divide students into groups of 12 to 15. Have students stand in a circle and raise one hand. Have them reach into the center of the circle and grab the hand of someone who is not standing next to them. Then have them repeat with the other hand. Instruct them to make sure that they are not holding both hands with the same person. The task is to unknot themselves without letting go of either hand. (They may rotate their hands in their partner's hand, but not let go). Debrief by discussing what went well, what could have gone better, how different people took on leadership roles, and how students encouraged others to take on leadership roles.

- **Service project.** Have students work in groups to identify a service project. Ask them to define the goal of this project and the steps that need to be taken to achieve this goal. Have them discuss their strengths using the Strengths Questionnaire (p. 162) in order to decide who will be responsible for leading each step of the project.

- **Shared leadership.** Have students work in small groups of three to four students to find examples of shared leadership to present to the class.

Strengths Questionnaire

Ask the following questions of everyone in the group. You may find that some people may be strong in multiple areas, while others are more proficient in just one. Note who feels particular excitement around a certain area. Add additional questions as desired.

How comfortable are you with technology? What areas are you strongest in?

How are you as an organizer? Do you like to keep track of all the different pieces of a project? Do you like creating timelines?

Are you able to identify what needs to be done and keep others accountable for meeting the goals?

How skilled are you as a researcher? Do you enjoy finding answers to questions?

How good are you as a writer? Can you write clearly and concisely to convey relevant information? Do you enjoy crafting a beautiful sentence?

How good are you at creating presentations? Do you like pulling ideas together in a way that is understandable to others?

How artistic are you? What are your preferred mediums? (e.g., music, theatre, etc.)

Do you prefer working with people or working more on tasks by yourself?

Do you enjoy tasks that are more creative or more structured?

Journal Prompts

Choose one or more of the journal prompts appropriate for the age level you work with. Feel free to modify or extend the prompt. Give students time to reflect on the questions in a personal journal. To extend the exercise, ask students to share their reflections with a peer or small group.

- Identify your own strengths using the Strengths Questionnaire (p. 162) as a guide. Add any strengths that you have that are not included in this questionnaire. Based on these strengths, what would be a good leadership role for you to have in a group?

- Identify three classmates who are not typically thought of as leaders. What are some of their strengths? How might you encourage them to take on leadership roles in group work?

- Think about a character in a book or movie that is an encouraging leader. What makes them encouraging? What are some outcomes of them being an encouraging leader?

- What is the benefit of shared leadership? What are some of the challenges with shared leadership?

- Do you encourage others to be leaders? What might you lose by encouraging others to be leaders? What might you gain?

Integrating the Attribute into Your Curriculum

Choose an activity from your planning guide or syllabus. After your students complete the activity, relate the activity back to the "encouraging" attribute with a debriefing conversation. Below are suggested questions. Choose or modify questions based on your students' developmental level, your activity, and your context.

This debrief can take the form of a full-group discussion. You might consider giving students time to reflect on their answers with partners or in small groups before asking them to share responses with the larger group. Alternatively, you may decide to ask students to work in small groups to share their responses on flip charts, and then have a gallery walk where students walk around the room and read what other students have written, potentially adding their own comments or thoughts.

- How did the activity help you understand the attribute "encouraging"?

- How did you work on being encouraging during this activity?

- How did other students demonstrate being encouraging during the activity?

- What does it mean to be encouraging?

- Why is it important to be encouraging?

- How can being encouraging make you a better leader?

- How can a lack of being encouraging impact leadership?

- How can you work on becoming a more encouraging leader?

- What are some ways you could practice being encouraging moving forward?

- How will you demonstrate being encouraging in your interactions with others?

- What impact can increasing your ability to be encouraging have on you?

- Identify a person, past or present, who demonstrates being encouraging. What specific actions does this person do that demonstrate being encouraging?

- Identify a book character who demonstrates being encouraging. What specific actions does this character do that demonstrate being encouraging?

Questions to Assess Understanding

Consider giving the following questions to students to determine if you need to spend more time explaining this attribute.

- What does it mean to be an encouraging leader? Give an example of someone you know who is an encouraging leader. How does this person demonstrate being an encouraging leader?

- What are three things you are going to work on in order to become a more encouraging leader?

Suggested Books to Introduce "Encouraging" ————

The books listed below can be used to deepen younger students' understanding of the "encouraging" attribute.

- *The Kissing Hand* by A. Penn

- *Miss Brooks Loves Books! (and I don't)* by B. Bottner

- *The Invisible Boy* by T. Ludwig & P. Barton

- *You Can Encourage Others: Tease or Inspire?* by C.C. Miller & V. Assanelli

Additional Resources

This section provides additional places to look for help and advice to develop your personal knowledge, as an adult, about this attribute.

Genett, D. M. (2004). *If you want it done right, you don't have to do it yourself! The power of effective delegation.* Fresno, CA: Quill Driver Books.

Krohe, J., Jr. (2010). *If you love your people, set them free.* Conference Board Review, 47(5), 28–37.

Kouzes, J. M., & Posner, B. Z. (1998). *Encouraging the heart: A leader's guide to rewarding and recognizing others.* San Francisco, CA: Jossey-Bass.

Ramsey, B., & Ramsey, D. (2018). *The leadership push: How to motivate extraordinary performance from ordinary workers.* Troy, IL: Morgan Laney Publishing.

Tracy, B. (2013). *Delegation and supervision.* New York, NY: American Management Association.

Turregano, C. (2013). *Delegating effectively: A leader's guide to getting things done.* Greensboro, NC: Center for Creative Leadership.

Young, J. (2014). *Encouragement in the Classroom.* Association for Supervision and Curriculum Development.

"Being confident means being a leader without being bossy."

– Fourth Grade Student

Chapter 14
CONFIDENT

• • •

"Being confident means believing in yourself and sharing your ideas."
– Sixth Grade Student

"[Confidence] means that someone works well with others, and gives their input, and they respect the people around them."
– 11th Grade Student

Introduction

Use the information in this section to help you introduce the "confident" attribute to students. You can use the question stem "How does this attribute make you a better leader?" to start a discussion with your students and to check for comprehension (see Additional Resources for more information to further your personal understanding).

Explaining "Confident" to Students

You don't need a title in order to be a leader, but you do need confidence—the belief that you have the ability to influence outcomes. How often have you been in a situation where there was a need for somebody to lead? How often do you voluntarily take on that leadership role? **Confident means stepping up and taking charge *when it is needed*.** This does not mean that you are the person who is always telling others what to do. Confident leaders listen to others and speak up as appropriate to help with direction, alignment, or commitment (DAC) (*see **Chapter 5: Collaborative** for more about DAC*). Confident leaders are self-assured and set a personal example of integrity, courage, and initiative. They act in a way that is consistent with their values, they are not afraid to stand up for what they believe, and they are able to lead action without hesitation when necessary. Your confidence is reflected through the way you carry yourself, the image you project, and your daily actions. If you are confident, then you are aware of how you can impact a situation, and you take the necessary steps to have positive impact. Confident leaders inspire commitment and a belief that things can get done. When confident leaders speak, people listen. When confident leaders act, people join in. Confident leaders are self-assured and not threatened by others, which allows them to listen to diverse opinions and thoughts.

What "Confident" Looks Like

Confident leaders:

- project self-assurance and poise

- command attention and respect

- are optimistic and take the attitude that most problems can be solved

- set a positive personal example

- accept setbacks with grace

- tolerate stressful situations and do not overreact

- communicate credibility

- avoid alienating people or damaging relationships

- rarely criticize other people

- are not easily rattled, distracted, or intimidated

- act with integrity

- share their thoughts and opinions

- listen to others' thoughts and opinions

- build trust with others

- are decisive when necessary

- contribute to the outcomes of direction, alignment, and commitment

What Gets in the Way?

If you are not confident, then you may have the tendency either to try to control others or to let others always take control. Read the following list and note the items that might be keeping you from being a confident leader *due to a desire to control others*.

- You tell people what to do without doing it yourself.

- You do not listen to others.

- You dominate conversations.

- You are overconfident.

- You are manipulative.

- You do not act in accordance with your core values or beliefs.

- You think your ideas are better or more important than anyone else's.

- You take control of a situation even if someone else is better suited to lead.

Read the following list and note the items that might be keeping you from being a confident leader *due to a desire to let others take control*.

- You lack self-assurance.

- You are afraid to speak up.

- You are worried you will be teased or judged about your ideas.

- You have difficulties dealing with stressful situations.

- You do not recognize when leadership is needed.

- You are afraid to take risks.

- You do not step up, even when you know there is a need for action.

Having the ability to step up and take charge when necessary, without trying to control every situation, will help you be a more effective social-emotional leader.

Suggestions for Improving "Confident"

Work with your students to discuss and establish some ways to build competency in this attribute. Below is a list to help support this exercise. Feel free to develop your own strategies or modify these suggestions.

You may also consider doing an activity with your students (see Activity Center for suggestions) or asking them to write about the attribute (see Journal Prompts for suggestions) to help build student understanding.

In conjunction with your students, figure out how you are going to support each other as a group or class to build competency in this leadership attribute.

- **Be clear.** Know what you want to communicate, and communicate it clearly. Vague, contradictory, or disjointed messages will likely leave others bored, confused, and feeling negative about your leadership. Conversely, a clear message enhances your ability to make a difference and inspire others.

- **Monitor your voice.** If what you're saying is valuable, how you say it is just as important. A leader with a flat or monotone vocal style, inappropriate volume, or poor diction will fail to inspire others.

- **Think "we."** By simply exchanging the words "I," "me," and "my" with more inclusive terms, you can foster a sense of community and gain trust. This will also help others recognize your collaborative spirit.

- **Lighten up.** Leaders don't need to be overly serious for others to take them seriously. An upbeat attitude and a kind word can lift the mood of those around you.

- **Exude energy.** Passion is contagious, and an energetic leader can motivate others to be their best.

- **Focus on managing stressful situations.** Responding poorly in times of stress or conflict will make others see you as a less confident leader.

- **Look in the mirror.** How might your body language display confidence? Be aware of how you sit and stand (your posture) when you are talking to others.

- **Seek a mentor.** Look for someone who can give you feedback and ideas about how you can be more confident. Build a partnership with this person—what can you teach them in exchange?

- **Show humility.** There is strength in vulnerability. Admitting that you make mistakes and taking accountability for them in a genuine way, with grace and a sincere commitment to improve, can boost others' perceptions of your leadership.

Activity Center

Here are some suggestions for activities that may be modified to fit your context and the students with whom you are working.

- **Book introduction.** Find a book to read with students that has a character who demonstrates the attribute "confident" or who would have benefitted from being more confident, and have students discuss or journal about the character's behavior (see the Suggested Books section of this chapter for books that could be used for this activity).

- **The Center of the Circle.** Have students stand in a circle, and have one student start in the middle of the circle. This person is the leader. The person in the center does a movement (such as waving their hands in the air) that everyone else replicates. Once the student in the center is sure that everyone is doing the same movement, they switch places with someone on the outside of the circle. Everyone continues to do that movement until the new leader gets into the middle of the circle and begins a new movement (such as snapping their fingers), then everyone follows this movement. This process continues until everyone has had a turn in the center of the circle. Nobody can go twice. Debrief with the following questions: How did it feel to be in the leadership role? How did you feel when you knew you were about to go into the center of the circle? How did it feel to give up your leadership role? What did you learn about yourself from this activity?

- **Birthdate.** Have students get into groups of 10 to 12. The task is for students to arrange themselves in order by birth date from youngest to oldest (paying attention to day, month, and year) within each of these groups. Debrief with the following questions: Who took charge during this activity in each group? How did they take charge? Why were they able to take charge? How did students lead with confidence?

- **Ted Talks.** Show the Ted Talk "What adults can learn from kids" by Adora Svitak (https://www.ted.com/talks/adora_svitak?language=en). Sample questions for discussion: How does Adora display confidence (both with words and body language)? How can you inspire confidence in others?

- **Over and under-confident leadership.** There is a fine line between taking too much control and too little control. Have students work in small groups to create scenes that show the impact of a student who takes too much control or too little control. Debrief these scenes with conversations about how confident leadership could have changed the outcome. Then reenact the scene with a confident leader who makes a positive impact.

- **Confident leaders.** Have students find examples of confident leaders, past or present, and explain why this individual is a confident leader (example: Rosa Parks). Make sure students discuss how this individual shows self-assurance, integrity, courage, and initiative.

- **Rotating leadership.** Make sure that at some point during the year every student has the opportunity to take a leadership role in the classroom.

Journal Prompts

Choose one or more of the journal prompts appropriate for the age level you work with. Feel free to modify or extend the prompt. Give students time to reflect on the questions in a personal journal. To extend the exercise, ask students to share their reflections with a peer or small group.

- What are some ways that you can work on becoming more confident?

- Describe a moment in which you displayed confident leadership. What did you do and how did others respond?

- When others reflect on this school year, how do you want others to describe you? What legacy do you want to leave behind?

- What are the three most visible actions you have taken in the last month? What might people conclude about you based on their observations of those actions?

- Think of someone who you believe is a confident leader. What does that person do to stand apart from others? How does this person's body language display confidence? How might you emulate their behavior in an authentic way?

- How did you handle the last stressful situation you found yourself in? How would you like to cope with stress? What could you do differently? How does stress affect your confidence?

Integrating the Attribute into Your Curriculum

Choose an activity from your planning guide or syllabus. After your students complete the activity, relate the activity back to the "confident" attribute with a debriefing conversation. Below are suggested questions. Choose or modify questions based on your students' developmental level, your activity, and your context.

This debrief can take the form of a full-group discussion. You might consider giving students time to reflect on their answers with partners or in small groups before asking them to share responses with the larger group. Alternatively, you may decide to ask students to work in small groups to share their responses on flip charts, and then have a gallery walk where students walk around the room and read what other students have written, potentially adding their own comments or thoughts.

- How did the activity that we did help you understand the attribute "confident"?

- How did you work on being confident during this activity?

- How did other students demonstrate being confident during the activity?

- What does it mean to be confident?

- Why is it important to be confident?

- How can being confident make you a better leader?

- How can a lack of being confident impact leadership?

- How can you work on becoming more confident?

- What are some ways you could practice being confident moving forward?

- How will you demonstrate being confident in your interactions with others?

- What impact can increasing your ability to be confident have on you?

- Identify a person, past or present, who demonstrates being confident. What specific actions demonstrate this person being confident?

- Identify a book character who demonstrates being confident. What specific actions does this character do that demonstrate being confident?

Questions to Assess Understanding

Consider giving the following questions to students to determine if you need to spend more time explaining this attribute.

- What does it mean to be a confident leader? Give an example of someone you know who is a confident leader. How does this person demonstrate being a confident leader?

- What are three things you are going to work on in order to become a more confident leader?

Suggested Books to Introduce "Confident"

The books listed below can be used to deepen younger students' understanding of the "confident" attribute.

- *Chrysanthemum* by K. Henkes

- *The Hero in Me* by S. Fitzsimonds & J. Covieo

- *I Am So Brave!* by S. Krensky

- *I Like Myself!* by K. Beaumont & D. Catrow

- *Leo's Gift* by S. Blackaby, J.T. Cicciarelli, & C. Schuler

- *The One, the Only Magnificent Me!* by D. Haseltine

- *Only One You* by L. Kranz

- *Purplicious* by E. Kann

- *The Story of Ferdinand* by M. Leaf

- *What Can a Citizen Do?* by D. Eggers & S. Harris

Additional Resources

This section provides additional places to look for help and advice to develop your personal knowledge, as an adult, about this attribute.

Booher, D. D. (1994). *Communicate with confidence! How to say it right the first time and every time.* New York, NY: McGraw-Hill.

Booher, D. D. (2011). *Creating personal presence: Look, talk, think, and act like a leader.* San Francisco, CA: Berrett-Koehler Publishers.

Criswell, C., & Campbell, D. (2008). *Building an authentic leadership image.* Greensboro, NC: Center for Creative Leadership.

Cuddy, A. J. C. (2015). *Presence: Bringing your boldest self to your biggest challenges.* New York, NY: Little, Brown and Company.

Kennedy-Moore, E. (2019). *Kid confidence: Help your child make friends, build resilience, and develop real self-esteem.* Oakland, CA: New Harbinger Publications.

Horth, D. M., Miller, L., & Mount, P. (2016). *Leadership brand: Deliver on your promise.* Greensboro, NC: Center for Creative Leadership.

McGonigal, K. (2012). *The willpower instinct: How self-control works, why it matters, and what you can do to get more of it.* New York, NY: Avery.

Siegel, D. J., & Bryson, T. P. (2018). *The yes brain: How to cultivate courage, curiosity, and resilience in your child.* New York, NY: Bantam.

Conclusion

Through choosing to focus on student's social-emotional leadership, you have started to develop youth who are in charge of themselves and their own actions (Leading Self), youth that are able to work well with their peers (Leading with Others), and youth who have the skills to build a better future (Changing Your World). In developing competence in the fourteen leadership attributes, youth will be able to engage and motivate others to face the complex challenges of the 21st century.

About the Authors

Micela Leis

Micela Leis is a research associate in the Insights and Impact group at the Center for Creative Leadership. She leads research and evaluation for K-12 clients, especially in the areas of design and evaluation of school culture change. Her main focus of study is on the importance of trust in adult school communities. She led the development of the *Leadership Indicator for Students*, a tool for examining youth leadership in schools and youth-focused organization. This work was driven by her prior experience as an elementary school teacher. She holds a BA from Tufts University and a PhD in Education from the University of Virginia.

Susan Reinecke

As a CCL faculty member, Susan designs and delivers custom-designed leadership solutions that include both short-term experiences and systemic initiatives. Her experiences as a professional educator in public and private schools, community colleges, and universities give her an insider's perspective of the challenges and rewards of innovation for improving leadership for youth and adults. Susan holds an EdM in Human Development and Psychology from the Harvard University Graduate School of Education, an MFA in Interdisciplinary Arts from Goddard College, a MEd from University of North Carolina at Greensboro, and a BA from the University of North Carolina at Chapel Hill.

Acknowledgements

This book would not exist without the help and support of many individual contributors. To start, we would like to thank our Societal Advancement colleagues at the Center for Creative Leadership for their support of this work, especially Lynn Fick-Cooper, Michael DePass, Courtney Gentry, and Joel Wright. We would like to give a huge thank you to Marin Burton, Greg Cameron, Justin McCollum, and William Murphy for reading through different draft versions of this and providing edits and suggestions, and of course to our editors, Peter Scisco and Shaun Martin. We would also like to thank Amanda Fonorow and Amy Cox Cameron for their invaluable support with the Suggested Books and Additional Resources sections of the book.

We would like to thank our research collaborators whose efforts led to the creation of the Student Leadership Framework: specifically, Preston Yarborough, Tim Leisman, Chris Rehm, Nicholas Lindsay, Valerie Ehrlich, Jeff Kosovich, and Holly Downs. These colleagues contributed to our data analysis and framework development. We would also like to thank all of those who participated in our surveys and interviews, especially students, faculty, and parents at Ravenscroft School, in Raleigh, North Carolina, and Charlotte Latin School, in Charlotte, North Carolina. We also thank all of the public schools in Vermont, South Carolina, and North Carolina that participated in data collection for our pilot studies.

We gratefully acknowledge Peter Scisco, Elaine Biech, and George Hallenbeck, the authors of *Compass: Your Guide for Leadership Development and Coaching*. We couldn't have written this book without their initial vision and research. Last, but not least, the authors are sincerely grateful to all of the CCL faculty who have participated in the work of CCL since its founding in 1970.

About the Center for Creative Leadership

The Center for Creative Leadership (CCL) is a top-ranked, global provider of leadership development. By leveraging the power of leadership to drive results that matter most to clients, CCL transforms individual leaders, teams, organizations, and society. Our array of cutting-edge solutions is steeped in extensive research and experience gained from working with hundreds of thousands of leaders at all levels. Ranked among the world's top five providers of executive education by the *Financial Times* and in the top 10 by *Bloomberg Businessweek*, CCL has offices in Greensboro, North Carolina; Colorado Springs, Colorado; San Diego, California; Brussels, Belgium; Moscow, Russia; Addis Ababa, Ethiopia; Johannesburg, South Africa; Singapore; Gurgaon, India; and Shanghai, China. For more information, visit www.ccl.org.

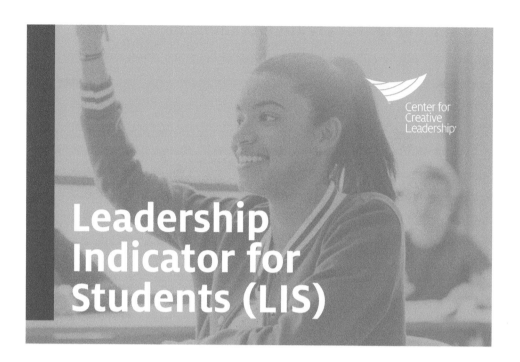

Leadership Indicator for Students (LIS)

The dimensions and attributes of student leadership described in this book can be measured by the Leadership Indicator for Students (LIS). LIS is a short, online CCL assessment that can be used to understand where to direct student leadership efforts by focusing on the gaps between the leadership attributes viewed as most important and students' strengths in those attributes.

The LIS also helps create a common understanding and language of leadership to support consistent developmental efforts in the areas most important to student outcomes.

This validated assessment is available in three versions: one for K-12 schools, one for youth-serving organizations, and one for higher education institutions.

To view a sample report or purchase the LIS, visit https://solutions.ccl.org/leadership-indicator-for-students.